Cambridge Elements

Elements in the Global Middle Ages
edited by
Geraldine Heng
University of Texas at Austin
Susan J. Noakes
University of Minnesota–Twin Cities
Lynn Ramey
Vanderbilt University

ISLAMICATE ENVIRONMENTS

Water, Land, Plants, and Society

D. Fairchild Ruggles
University of Illinois at Urbana-Champaign

Shaftesbury Road, Cambridge CB2 8EA, United Kingdom

One Liberty Plaza, 20th Floor, New York, NY 10006, USA

477 Williamstown Road, Port Melbourne, VIC 3207, Australia

314–321, 3rd Floor, Plot 3, Splendor Forum, Jasola District Centre, New Delhi – 110025, India

103 Penang Road, #05–06/07, Visioncrest Commercial, Singapore 238467

Cambridge University Press is part of Cambridge University Press & Assessment, a department of the University of Cambridge.

We share the University's mission to contribute to society through the pursuit of education, learning and research at the highest international levels of excellence.

www.cambridge.org
Information on this title: www.cambridge.org/9781009483407

DOI: 10.1017/9781009483384

© D. Fairchild Ruggles 2025

This publication is in copyright. Subject to statutory exception and to the provisions of relevant collective licensing agreements, no reproduction of any part may take place without the written permission of Cambridge University Press & Assessment.

When citing this work, please include a reference to the DOI 10.1017/9781009483384

First published 2025

A catalogue record for this publication is available from the British Library

ISBN 978-1-009-48340-7 Hardback
ISBN 978-1-009-48341-4 Paperback
ISSN 2632-3427 (online)
ISSN 2632-3419 (print)

Cambridge University Press & Assessment has no responsibility for the persistence or accuracy of URLs for external or third-party internet websites referred to in this publication and does not guarantee that any content on such websites is, or will remain, accurate or appropriate.

Islamicate Environments

Water, Land, Plants, and Society

Elements in the Global Middle Ages

DOI: 10.1017/9781009483384
First published online: February 2025

D. Fairchild Ruggles
University of Illinois at Urbana-Champaign

Author for correspondence: D. Fairchild Ruggles, dfr1@illinois.edu

Abstract: Islam burst forth from Arabia in the seventh century and spread with astonishing speed and force into the Middle East, Asia, and northern Africa and the Mediterranean. While its success as a dominant culture has often been attributed to military strength, astute political organization, and religious factors, this Element focuses on the environmental conditions from which early Islamic societies sprang. In the belt of arid land that stretches from Iran to the Maghreb (Spain and Morocco) – that is, the territories of early Islam – the adaptation of natural water systems, landforms and plant varieties was required to make the land habitable and productive.

Keywords: technology, agriculture, irrigation, Islamic culture, New Materialism

© D. Fairchild Ruggles 2025

ISBNs: 9781009483407 (HB), 9781009483414 (PB), 9781009483384 (OC)
ISSNs: 2632-3427 (online), 2632-3419 (print)

Contents

Prefatory Note — 1

1 The Formation of the Islamic Environment — 1

2 Technology: Water from Below — 22

3 Technology: Water from Above — 39

4 Technology: The *Qanat* — 58

5 Irrigation Societies and Agricultural Expertise — 75

6 Conclusion: An Environmental Perspective on the Islamicate Mediterranean — 83

Bibliography — 91

Acknowledgements — 101

Prefatory Note

All dates are common era.

Arabic diacritics are used only in the first instance where an Arabic or Berber term is introduced, and are not used for personal names, places, or the titles of texts.

1 The Formation of the Islamic Environment

Islam burst forth on the Arabian Peninsula in the seventh century and spread with astonishing speed from Mecca and Medina to Syria and the eastern Mediterranean, eastward beyond Iraq and Iran to the Indus River valley, and westward to Egypt, Tunisia, Morocco and Algeria (known in Islam as the Maghreb), and the Iberian Peninsula (known as al-Andalus), together forming the *dār al-Islām* (equivalent to the modern term "the Islamic world") (Figure 1). Even as the political unity of Islam fragmented in the tenth century, with different caliphates ruling from Baghdad, Kairouan (and Cairo), and Cordoba, it retained cultural coherence. Its rapid expansion and success as a dominant culture has often been attributed to astute political organization, military strength, and religious factors that facilitated conversion to Islam, these leading to prosperity despite having to overcome adverse environment conditions. However, while it is true that the belt of land that stretches from Iran to the Maghreb mostly consisted of sparsely settled desert inhabited by nomadic herders and traders rather than farmers (Figure 2), under Islamic rule the adaptation of natural water sources for irrigation made the land increasingly habitable for settled populations as well as increasingly suitable for growing an array of crops. Moreover, because the climate was similar from one end of the Mediterranean to the other, any innovations or improvements to the human-land relationship in one area could be transported to another relatively easily. The resultant agricultural productivity yielded not simply abundance but excess, stimulating trade that supported the expansion of market centers and a highly literary urban culture.

The agricultural expansion and the wealth it generated allowed the arts to flourish, including the garden, which is acclaimed as a major cultural development in regions under Islamic rule. Although a common approach to Islamic landscape history is to assert an all-encompassing religious framework and attribute garden form and meaning to the passages in the Quran that describe paradise as a garden, this Cambridge Element moves between an environmental history approach and New Materialism. Focusing on water and hydraulic systems as primary environmental challenges and opportunities, it examines the various forms of agency held by farmers and the way that the environment

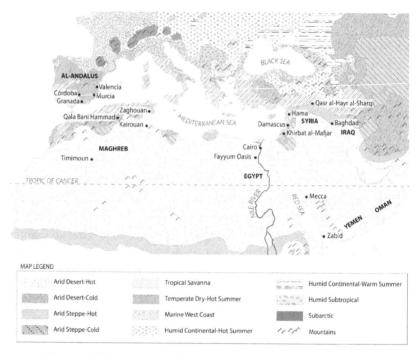

Figure 1 Climate map with named sites (drawing: M. Mallula)

Figure 2 Libyan Desert (photo: Luca Galuzzi)

imposes conditions to which humankind, and farmers of the premodern period in particular, must adapt.

The initial questions begin with the harnessing of existing Roman and Persian technologies, the importation and dissemination of new plant varieties, and the recording of agronomic and botanical knowledge in scientific treatises, asking how these strengthened the economy and contributed to a culture that celebrated the garden as a major art form.[1] But thereafter, instead of focusing on the design of a select group of gardens, this Element explores the landscape as a managed system in which a balance can be observed between the human (seen in the way that things such as law, taxation, and timekeeping pertain to the land) and the natural (seen in the climate, existing water sources, and native plant species).

The argument will focus on the environmental conditions of the Islamic Mediterranean and the Middle East in the early period, defined here as extending from the seventh through the twelfth century. Because there is a lot of agronomic information for Yemen, Egypt, and the Iberian Peninsula, those regions receive the most attention. The term "Islamic" will serve to indicate those lands under Muslim political rule in which Islamic law and culture predominated, but the term "Islamicate" will also be used to describe cultural practices where Islamic culture prevailed but where communities of other faiths – Christian and Jewish, among others – also flourished. Regardless of their religious identity, the people of such communities might speak Arabic, Persian or other languages and might engage in the same pursuit of scientific knowledge or experience the same delight in a beautiful Arabic poem. This kind of cultural diversity occurred especially in regions where the Islamic state governed a majority population of non-Muslims, as in the Iberian Peninsula and South Asia, and it also occurred at the scale of the family, where Muslim men might have non-Muslim wives or concubines. In such unions, non-Muslim women were not required to convert to Islam, and one can imagine the ensuing domestic cultural complexity, reflected in cooking, music, and speech.

Just as the words for various foods are usually regionally specific, water and land terminology varies from region to region. The water lever that is known as a *shādūf* in one place is called a *khaṭṭāra* in another. The underground aqueduct known as the *qanāt* in central Islamic lands was known as the *foggara* (*fuqāra*) in the Maghreb.[2] Waterwheels are variously known as *nāʿūra*, *sāqīya*, and *dulāb*. In light of this, I will not try to supply all the local names here but

---

[1] D. F. Ruggles, *Islamic Gardens and Landscapes* (Philadelphia: University of Pennsylvania Press, 2008).

[2] A. Wilson, "Classical Water Technology in the Early Islamic World," in C. Bruun and A. Saastamoinen (eds.), *Technology, Ideology, Water: From Frontinus to the Renaissance and beyond* (Acta Instituti Romani Finlandiae, 31) (Rome, 2004), 126 n. 54.

instead will provide that which appears most often in the descriptive and analytical literature.

As a conquering culture, early Islam built upon Roman and Sasanian precedents as well as preexisting indigenous practices that had flourished without imperial oversight. Moreover, just as Islam encouraged and facilitated religious conversion and absorbed a wide variety of new peoples into its fold through marriage and slavery, it also adopted an eclectic approach to cultural difference, borrowing and adapting new practices and forms of knowledge, including mathematics and the natural sciences learned from Greek and Latin texts, and new forms of architecture, such as the Roman dome and the Sasanian *iwān* (a great apsidal vault, open on one side). The eclecticism is very apparent in agriculture, where early Muslim farmers observed and readily adopted technologies from Roman precedents: like the Romans, they built canals and aqueducts to transport water, constructed large waterwheels to raise it from places of storage, and cultivated the basic triad of wheat, olives, and grapes. Moreover, in many areas of the Mediterranean, Roman infrastructure such as roads, aqueducts, and bridges was reused under Muslim rule and served as the model for new construction. In 698, for example, Muslims revived the second-century Roman aqueduct that ran from a monumental spring-fed nymphaeum in Zaghouan (Tunisia) to supply the cisterns of Carthage.[3] In the mid-eighth century, the palace of Khirbat al-Mafjar (near Jericho), which seems to have occupied the position of a much older Roman fortress, was supplied by a Roman aqueduct that continued in use, bringing water from a nearby spring.[4]

Modes of Agricultural Production

However, if the Muslims readily adopted pre-existing infrastructure and technology in the lands they conquered, they developed very different patterns of settlement. This is evident in Baetica province, in the southern part of the Iberian Peninsula (which under Islamic rule became al-Andalus), one of the most productive agricultural regions in the Roman Empire from the first to early third century CE. The Roman agricultural landscape was characterized by latifundia, large estates which, because of their size and value, belonged to the wealthiest echelon of society. The estates, which were concentrated along

---

[3] A. Wilson, "Water Supply in Ancient Carthage," in J. T. Peña, J. J. Rossiter, A. I. Wilson et al. (eds.), *Carthage Papers* (*Journal of Roman Archaeology*, Supplementary series 28) (Portsmouth, RI, 1998), 65–102.

[4] R. W. Hamilton, *Khirbat al-Mafjar: An Arabian Mansion in the Jordan Valley* (Oxford: Clarendon Press, 1959); D. Whitcomb, M. Jennings, A. Creekmore, and I. Arce, "Khirbet al-Mafjar: New Excavations and Hypotheses for an Umayyad Monument," *Near Eastern Archaeology* 79.2 (2016): 78–87.

Islamicate Environments

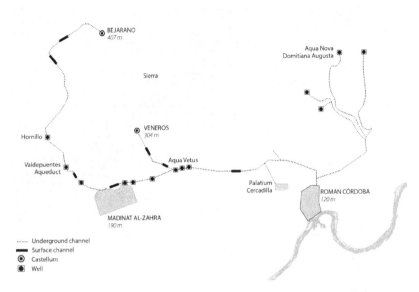

Figure 3 Cordoba's Roman water system (drawing: M. Mallula and D.F. Ruggles)

the Guadalquivir River, stretching from Cordoba to Seville, took advantage of ideal conditions in that fertile valley. The river itself was an asset, not because it provided irrigation water – running below the ground level of the farms, it was actually an inconvenient source – but because it provided a transportation artery that allowed agricultural products to be easily shipped out to the Mediterranean.

As an alluvial plain, the soils along the Guadalquivir were naturally fertile, rich in organic material and minerals. The Romans largely practiced dryland farming, and to the extent that irrigation was needed for household use and kitchen gardens, it was provided by the foothills of the Sierra Morena from which seasonal streams flowed down to the farms during the growing season, which began in the late fall and culminated in the spring. In situating their villas, the Romans did not venture past the naturally arable areas of the valley. Although they built impressive arched aqueducts throughout the Mediterranean, their purpose was to deliver water to cities, not rural areas. Indeed, in Cordoba a surface canal 24 kilometers in length brought water from the Sierra, splitting as it reached the city so that one branch entered Cordoba from the north and the other from the west (Figure 3).[5]

In contrast, Muslims managed much smaller plots of agricultural land, built water systems that served both urban and rural peoples, and invested extraordinary

---

[5] Á. Ventura Villanueva, *El Abastecimiento de agua a la Córdoba romana*, 2 vols. Volume 1: *El acueducto de Valdepuentes* (Cordoba: Universidad de Córdoba, 1993), 163–5.

labor in transforming the terrain to increase the amount of available space for cultivation. Whereas Roman latifundia relied on slave labor, under Islam land was customarily parceled out in small plots to individual farmers (who might also have slaves, albeit in far fewer numbers). The great historian Ibn Khaldun (1332–1406), remarking on the excellence of agriculture in al-Andalus, commented on the fact that the Andalusis were all farmers: "It rarely happens among them that a man in authority or an ordinary person has no tract of land or field, or does not do some farming."[6]

Oleson, in his study of Greek and Roman technology, placed great emphasis on this difference between the Roman and Muslim mindset in regard to labor. He proposed that the conceptual distance between the Roman landowner and the villa, in which work was entirely performed by slaves, was caused by a split between the Roman ruling class, who liked to debate the finer points of philosophy and who admired the life of the mind, and all the rest who engaged in mundane work. In sum, Roman landowners preferred literature over the practical sciences, with the result that innovation suffered.[7] In contrast, the landowner in the Islamic world was likely to know the land intimately and to have a keen eye for any improvement that might increase the farm's yield or reduce labor. Oleson all but overlooks the Roman literary tradition on agriculture, emblematized by Cato's *De Agricultura*, Varro's *De Re Rustica*, and Columella's *De Re Rustica* – and the Romans did manage to feed an entire empire, after all–but his point was that in the Roman imperial period (from 31 BCE onward) the conception and practice of farming occurred at a large scale.

This is not to say that all Andalusi farms were small. There were larger holdings as well – for example in the region of Murcia in eastern al-Andalus, land ownership ranged in size from small properties of less than a quarter of a hectare (about a half an acre) to those that exceeded one hectare – however, Islamic practice assumed that land was not held by a distant lord and farmed by slaves or serfs who lacked autonomy, but by someone who lived on or near the land that he or she cultivated.[8] Therefore, if yields could be improved by building a temporary dam across a mountain stream to capture and distribute water for irrigation, as occurred in the Yemeni highlands, or by digging a system of canals to bring water from mountain sources to farmland below, as occurred in Granada (Spain), the gains from the higher yields thus generated

---

[6] Ibn Khaldun, *The Muqaddimah: An Introduction to History*, trans. F. Rosenthal (Princeton: Princeton University Press, 1967), 278.

[7] J. P. Oleson, *Greek and Roman Mechanical Water-Lifting Devices: The History of a Technology* (Dordrecht: D. Reidl, 1984), 399–401; citing H. W. Pleket, "Technology and Society in the Graeco-Roman World," *Acta Historiae Neerlandica* 2 (1967): 1–25.

[8] C. Trillo San José, "A Social Analysis of Irrigation in Al-Andalus: Nazari Granada (13th–15th centuries)," *Journal of Medieval History* 31 (2005): 163–83, see esp. 170.

were likely to be perceived by that local owner right away and reinvested in the immediate area.

Muslim social structure may account for some of the difference in the modes of production. With respect to Iraq, one historian has explained the relative freedom of the Muslim farmer as stemming from a nomadic legacy.[9] But a more persuasive explanation is that these settled communities were organized according to clan. In rural areas of the early Islamic world, landowners usually lived in communities of kin or with strong neighborly relationships. They were not feudal serfs, but nor were they entirely free agents when it came to making decisions about their land. There was some mobility, but property, when exchanged, was more likely to be sold to a family member or acquired through marriage (marriages arranged precisely to facilitate such consolidation of holdings) than sold on the open market. Therefore land, and the water rights that often went with it, was much more than a commodity; it represented a complex network of social relations. Indeed, by tracking the changing ownership of land in a hamlet such as those in the Alpujarra region of Spain, one can track social shifts such as the gradual move away from the traditional cousin marriages, which kept property within the same clan, to exogenous marriages, in which wealthy families sought marriages with un-related families of equal wealth to improve their economic position.[10]

Shaping the Land

Because of the enormous labor required, neither the Romans nor their Muslim successors would seek to alter the contours of the lands they farmed unless there was a clear benefit in doing so. However, in mountainous areas, dramatic land transformation was sometimes necessary to take advantage of water supplies and enable farming in areas that were otherwise inhospitable to it. Long predating the arrival of Islam, the Nabataeans, who lived in the Levant and northern portion of the Arabian Peninsula from the fourth century BCE to 106 CE, cut terraces into the hillsides on the outskirts of Petra to create stepped horizontal plots that could be farmed. The interventions at Petra were undertaken a bit more than a century before the Nabataeans were formally brought into the Roman world in 106 CE.[11] Thereafter, successive Byzantine and Muslim communities continued to farm the terraces and maintain the water

---

[9] H. Q. El-Samarraie, *Agriculture in Iraq during the 3rd Century, A.H.* (Beirut: Librairie du Liban, 1972).

[10] Trillo San José, "A Social Analysis of Irrigation," 174.

[11] A. R. Knodell, S. E. Alcock, C. A. Tuttle et al., "The Brown University Petra Archaeological Project: Landscape Archaeology in the Northern Hinterland of Petra, Jordan," *American Journal of Archaeology* 121.4 (2017): 621–83.

Figure 4 Terraced highlands, Yemen (photo: Hemis/Alamy)

systems for the next millennium. Similarly in Yemen, where the slope of the land in the mountainous areas of the southern coasts can reach 35 degrees, but where those same mountains provided a reliable source of natural water runoff, land was likewise terraced to create horizontal plots for agriculture (Figure 4). Although terracing is difficult to date, scholars estimate that most of the terracing in Yemen predated Islam by a thousand (possibly as much as three thousand) years.[12] Owing nothing to Roman engineering, the technique was part of an indigenous legacy inherited by later Muslim farmers. Indeed, the fact that historians regularly point to Roman origins for the agricultural systems that would be adopted under Islam is misleading because in many regions – such as the Maghreb – the systems seem to have been developed by local inhabitants as a way of coping with local conditions.

In the mountains east of Granada, in the region known as the Alpujarra, the mountain slopes are heavily terraced. Although the precise dating of the land transformation is not known, it is likely to be the work of Berbers, who came from the Maghreb to settle the area in the eleventh and twelfth centuries. As the investment would not have been worthwhile without the canals (called *acequias* in Spain) that brought water to the terraces, the terraces must date to the period

---

[12] T. Wilkinson, "Settlement, Soil Erosion and Terraced Agriculture in Highland Yemen: A Preliminary Statement," in *Proceedings of the Seminar for Arabian Studies* (Papers from the Thirty-Second meeting of the Seminar for Arabian Studies held in London, July 16–18, 1998) 29 (1999): 183–91.

Figure 5 Aerial view of Madinat al-Zahra' (photo: stu.dio/Alamy)

when the canal system was built between the twelfth century and the late fifteenth century, corresponding to the periods of Zirid and Nasrid rule, after which Granada was conquered by the armies of Isabel and Ferdinand. The construction of horizontal landforms buttressed by stone walls, together with the building up of the soil through fertilization and the removal of stones, was labor and capital intensive. But the plots of land made in this manner were even more fertile that other irrigated terrain because the terrace walls prevented runoff and trapped a thick layer of good soil.[13]

In the Islamic world, terracing could also be an architectural enhancement, as in the elite estates built outside of Cordoba in the tenth century. The architects of the caliphal palatine city Madinat al-Zahra' (which lasted from 936 to 1010) carved three stepped levels into the foot of the mountain from which water was transported through the remains of a much older Roman hydraulic system that had been built to serve the city of Cordoba (Figure 5). Although not primarily an agricultural site, the palace was reported to have fig and almond trees that created a brilliant splash of white in the landscape when in bloom.[14] In describing the palace, medieval writers such as al-'Udhri, al-Idrisi, al-Nuwayri, and al-Himyari mentioned the extraordinary terraces, one of which was entirely

---

[13] T. D. Douglas, S. J. Kirkby, R. W. Critchley and G. J. Park et al., "Agricultural Terrace Abandonment in the Alpujarra, Andalucia, Spain," *Land Degradation & Rehabilitation* 5 (1994): 281–91.

[14] R. Dozy, G. Dugat, L, Krehl, and W. Wright, *Gardens, Landscape, and Vision in the Palaces of Islamic Spain* (University Park: Pennsylvania State University Press, 2000), 57; al-Maqqari, *Analectes sur l'histoire et la littérature des arabes d'Espagne*, ed. R. Dozy et al., 2 vols. in 3 (Leiden: E.J. Brill, 1855–1861; reprinted London: Oriental Press, 1967), I: 344.

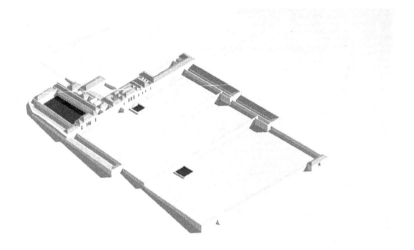

Figure 6 al-Rummaniyya (drawing: Felix Arnold/German Archaeological Institute)

occupied by a reception hall overlooking a vast garden with ornamental pools. Despite the high cost of leveling the three platforms that the sloping site necessitated, the selection of an elevated position facilitated the delivery of water from the mountains above and the stepped layout allowed the water to run easily through the various gardens, fountains, baths, and latrines. Nearby, the al-Rummaniyya estate likewise unfolded in stepped levels, the residential buildings, and a large tank of water on the highest level, with three terraces of orchards descending from there (Figure 6).[15] Although the focus here is on the mechanisms and reasons for sculpting the land in this way, in other publications I have more fully explored the profound symbolic meaning of the act of land transformation as a metaphor for sovereign power in which elevated terraces provided far-reaching vistas that became a sign for the sovereign's political territory.[16]

Plants

In addition to the ownership and management of the land, the practice of plant cultivation differed from the Roman to the Islamic period. To prevent soil exhaustion caused by the depletion of nitrogen, Roman farmers would apply

---

[15] F. Arnold, A. Canto García, and A. Vallejo Triano, *La almunia de Al-Rummāniyya (Córdoba)* (Sevilla: Consejería de Cultura [Junta de Andalucía], 2021).

[16] Ruggles, *Gardens, Landscape, and Vision*; D. F. Ruggles, "The Gardens of the Alhambra and the Concept of the Garden in Islamic Spain," in J. D. Dodds (ed.), *Al-Andalus: The Arts of Islamic Spain* (New York: Metropolitan Museum, 1992), 162–71.

animal manure as fertilizer and divide a field into two halves. They would cultivate one side for a season (lasting from fall until spring) and then would leave that side fallow for the next growing cycle and turn to cultivate the other side. This meant that any given plot of land was productive only once every two years.[17] Irrigation, careful plant selection, and more intensive application of a broader range of fertilizers could have eliminated the need for fallowing and doubled the yield, yet the Romans primarily grew dry crops that did not require extensive irrigation systems or other forms of augmentation. Nonetheless, Roman agriculture successfully produced a triad of staple crops: wheat, olive, and grape. Although domesticated through the centuries – and in Baetica, archaeological evidence indicates that the earliest olive trees were domesticated in the first millennium BCE – the plants largely came from wild origins. As native species, they were well suited to the farm environments in which they were improved through selection and grown on a large scale.[18] The olive has remained a key crop throughout Spain's history (Figure 7).

While the farmers in the Islamic period relied on the same basic crops, they also experimented with a wide variety of imported plants, the success of which was due to new agrarian practices. Andrew Watson's ground-breaking thesis of an "agricultural revolution" in early Islam showed that, due to a connected culture stretching from Central Asia to Yemen and the Mediterranean in the seventh century and onward, goods and ideas travelled westward. Among these were many plant species, of which he traced the routes of eighteen: Asiatic rice, sorghum, durum wheat, sugar cane, cotton, watermelon, eggplant, spinach, artichoke, taro root, sour orange, lemon, lime, banana, plantain, mango, coconut, and pomelo.[19]

When new specimens were brought from the East, either through trade, diplomatic gifts, or active pursuit – as documented in the case of a prized variety of fig smuggled into Cordoba in the ninth century – the local farmers were able to domesticate the exotic plants through adaptation of the soil, application of appropriate fertilizers, and irrigation.[20] Regarding the rotation of legume crops to replenish the soil, the Andalusian agronomist Ibn Luyun (1282–1349) clearly stated in his agricultural treatise that "beans, lupins, flax, and vetch [peas] are

---

[17] C. Trillo San José, *Agua y Paisaje en Granada* (Granada: Diputación de Granada, 2003), 12–13.
[18] O. Bourgeon, C. Pagnoux, S. Mauné, E. García Vargas et al., "Olive Tree Varieties Cultivated for the Great Baetican Oil Trade between the 1st and the 4th Centuries AD: Morphometric Analysis of Olive Stones from Las Delicias (Ecija, Province of Seville, Spain)," *Vegetation History and Archaeobotany* 27.3 (2018): 463–76, esp. 464; Trillo San José, *Agua y Paisaje en Granada*, 17.
[19] A. Watson, *Agricultural Innovation in the Early Islamic World: The Diffusion of Crops and Farming Techniques, 700–1100* (Cambridge: Cambridge University Press, 1983).
[20] J. Samsó, "Ibn Hišām al-Lajmī y el primer jardín botánico en al-Andalus," *Revista del Instituto Egipcio de Estudios Islámicos en Madrid* 21 (1981–1982): 140; E. García Gómez, "Sobre agricultura arábigo andaluza," *Al-Andalus* 10 (1945): 127–46.

Figure 7 Old olive trees grown on terraced land in the Alpujarra region of Spain (photo: D.F. Ruggles)

good for the soil. Millet and sesame and the repeated cultivation of anything debilitates it."[21] With a larger palette of food and fiber plants that could be cultivated, agriculture became more varied, and because irrigation, fertilization, and crop rotation allowed for multiple crops to be grown in one plot of land, an "agricultural revolution" transpired. The growth in the volume of crops as well as the ensuing resiliency that was afforded – one crop feeding the people when another failed, one type of plant succeeding in an ecological niche that was hostile to other cultivated plants – strengthened the economy and allowed trade

---

[21] Ibn Luyun, *Ibn Luyūn: Tratado de agricultura*, trans. J. Eguaras Ibáñez (Granada: Patronato de la Alhambra y Generalife, 1975; Almería: Editorial Universidad de Almería, 2014), folio 3r.

networks to proliferate. In this way, Watson traced a clear line from new plants to new techniques and technologies, to social change.[22]

In the early Islamic period, such plant migrations are well documented, often due to the patronage of rulers who delighted in collecting new flowers and plants, some of which stimulated the senses of smell and taste. Exotic varieties of fig and pomegranate as well as other fruit trees were brought to the Umayyad, taifa, and Almohad courts of al-Andalus where they were acculturated in experimental botanical gardens. Al-Andalus became famed for the diversity and high quality of its agricultural products and for its handsome gardens, which in their layout and fecundity seemed to represent the larger cultivated landscape.

In the Yemen, the Rasulid rulers (1229–1454) also had a keen interest in botanical acquisition. They obtained fruit trees from the Ayyubid sultan Saladin in the twelfth century, and their court historian, al-Khazraji (d. 1410), mentioned a diplomatic mission from Abyssinia and Calicut in 1263 that brought roses and jasmine, which the sultan immediately ordered to be cultivated in his own garden. An envoy in 1367 from Cambay and Sind brought three varieties of exotic pepper-tree plants, and two years later another visitor from Calicut brought "a quantity of curious plants and birds" that included white jasmine, yellow jasmine, and roses that were immediately planted in one of the sultan's gardens. In 1392, a new diplomatic envoy sent "various kinds of trees of his country, such as *Pandanus odoratissimus* [screw pine], sugar-canes, sapling myrtles, dark-flowering allium, dark-flowering bean, many varieties of grape, and other things."[23] It is important to note not only the great variety of trees and plants but also that so many of them came from elsewhere and that they were soon domesticated in the gardens of Yemen. The Rasulids' attention to horticulture and agriculture continued under their successors, the Tahirids (1454–1517).

An economic historian, Watson relied on Arabic texts rather than archaeology for evidence of the transmission of plants. In particular, he used the large corpus of calendars (agricultural almanacs), botanical treatises, and a type of farm manual known as a *kitāb al-filāḥa* ("book of agriculture") that have survived from Iraq, Spain, Egypt, Yemen, the Maghreb, Syria, and Iran. The Filaha Texts Project lists twenty-seven authors and texts, twenty-one of them

---

[22] An excellent assessment of the larger stakes of the argument and the lasting impact of Watson's work can be found in P. Squatriti, "Of Seeds, Seasons, and Seas: Andrew Watson's Medieval Agrarian Revolution Forty Years Later," *The Journal of Economic History* 74.4 (2014): 1205–20.

[23] D. Varisco, *Medieval Agriculture and Islamic Science: The Almanac of a Yemeni Sultan* (Seattle: University of Washington Press, 1994), 156–57; al-Khazraji, *The Pearl-Strings: A History of the Résuliyy Dynasty of Yemen*, ed. Muhammad ʿAsal, trans. J. W. Redhouse, 5 vols. (Leiden: Brill; London: Luzac, 1906–1919), 2: 118–20; I. Hehmeyer, *A History of Water Engineering and Management in Yemen* (Leiden: Brill, 2019), 64–5.

written before 1400, and its introductory essay provides the best comprehensive analysis of medieval Islamic farming as can be found anywhere.[24] If the website's list of *filaha* texts is not complete, it is in part because it can be difficult to differentiate between an agricultural manual, a calendar that serves as a farmer's almanac, and a calendar that may, in addition to information about the optimal sowing and harvest times for crops, also include information about the stars, the weather, food preservation, and animal husbandry. It also does not include key Greek and Roman texts that were translated into Arabic and circulated, such as *De materia medica*, a botanical dictionary of some 600 plants written by the Hellenistic physician Dioscorides in 78 CE.

Mirroring the east-west transmission of plants documented by Watson, an illustrated copy of *De materia medica* was sent from the Byzantine emperor in Constantinople to the Umayyad court in Cordoba in 948. Finding the Greek incomprehensible, Andalusi scholars set about providing a gloss of local names for the ones identified in the text. That multiple Arabic translations of the work were made for the Abbasid rulers in Baghdad and the Umayyad rulers in Cordoba, as well as later Latin and Spanish translations, is an indication of the great value placed on its information. The illustration (Figure 8) shows a leek, one of 769 illustrations from a Dioscorides manuscript that was made in Constantinople in the mid-tenth century at about the same time as the one sent to Cordoba. Evidence that this was read and glossed by an Arabic reader at some point in its history is given by the Arabic word *kurāth* (leek) lightly added below the plant's Greek name, which is written boldly in orange.

The goal of a botanical dictionary was more scientific than that of a *filaha* text. Written by medieval agronomists for literate readers, the Arabic agricultural manuals texts obviously do not fully represent the day-to-day chores of ordinary farmers, but nor were they entirely removed from actual practice. The eleventh-century Andalusi agronomist Abu'l-Khayr wrote in his explanation of the methods for propagating olive trees: "We have had the experience of doing this ourselves." Writing his *Kitab al-filaha* in the late twelfth century, Ibn al-Awwam assured his readers "I have recorded nothing in my work that I have not tried through experience many times." In a thirteenth-century treatise which was rhymed to optimize memorization, Ibn Luyun explained the method for getting rid of wasps by burning oil infused with garlic, saying, "This is a proven procedure," and elsewhere exhorted his reader "You should try this."[25]

---

[24] www.filaha.org

[25] Abu'l-Khayr, *Kitab al-Filahaa ou Le Livre de la Culture: Notice et extraits traduits par A. Cherbonneau, éclaircissements par H. Pérès*, ed. A. Cherbonneau and H. Pérès (Alger: Carbonel, 1946), 15; see also The Filaha Texts Project, https://filaha.org/khayr_final_translation_revised.html; Ibn al-Awwam, *Libro de Agricultura*, ed. J. I. Cubiero Salmerón from the

Islamicate Environments 15

Figure 8 Dioscorides, *De materia medica*, image of a leek (courtesy: the Morgan Library & Museum. MS M.652. Purchased by J.P. Morgan, 1920)

In the past, many of the scholars studying the agricultural manuals, including myself, have assumed that the manuals could not have been written for the farmers in the field.[26] And yet everything about these texts – their attention to the most minute detail, from growing plants to thwarting grubs, and the testimonials of the writers themselves – tells us that they were written to serve actual farmers and that their authors were close observers and even practitioners of the methods they described. The artificial division between the laboring farmer and an elite class of individuals who logically *must* have stood at a distance from

---

1802 translation by J. A. Banqueri (S.L.: Empresa Pública para el Desarrollo Agrario y Pesquero de Andalucía, 1999), prologue (p. 78); Ibn Luyun, *Tratado de agricultura*, numbers 61 and 36.

[26] Ruggles, *Gardens, Landscape, and Vision*, 27.

agricultural labor is a reflection not of early Islamicate culture but of the modern world where those who write do not usually plow. But the distinction is false because, as Ibn Khaldun noted previously, *all* the Andalusis were farmers. The assumption that the texts were written solely by and for the elite is predicated on the assumption of a "dumb peasant." However, in the design of irrigation systems, the mastery of the skill of leveling the earth, and establishment of authoritative bodies who could arbitrate disputes over land and water, it is very clear that peasant farmers were in fact highly knowledgeable and well-attuned to the environment in which they operated. This is not to argue for universal literacy or an active book culture among Andalusi farmers – indeed, most texts were disseminated by reading them aloud to their audiences – but to suggest that the stakes of successful, well-informed farming were understood at all levels of society.

In addition to identifying plants that were grown regionally and describing their cultivation, the agricultural texts describe the means of propagating those plants, the properties of the different kinds of soil, the wide variety of fertilizers that were used, and methods for food preservation. For this reason, as the Filaha Texts Project argues, the books are better characterized as books of husbandry. Collectively, the *filaha* texts provide a window onto botanical and agronomical sciences and even food culture of the first eight centuries of Islam. For the modern reader, they reveal "what we would now call an ecological sensibility, a holistic approach to farming and a duty of care towards nature that is implicit in the notion of husbandry as the prudent management and conservation of resources."[27]

Since the publication of Watson's book, some of the plants that he claimed as new introductions have been shown to have a pre-Islamic history in the Middle East and Mediterranean region; for example, watermelon and durum wheat. But for lemon, lime, sour orange, pomelo, sugarcane, sorghum, banana and plantain, and eggplant, others, archaeobotanical research has provided support for his thesis.[28] Moreover, even when shifting the timeline of the migration to an earlier period, most researchers acknowledge the veracity of his claim that the cultivation of these plants was greatly expanded under Islam and that the ability to expand the palette of available species was enabled by a concerted effort to provide irrigation.

---

[27] Filaha Texts Project, citing L. Bolens, *Les méthodes culturales au moyen âge d'après les traités d'agronomie andalous: Traditions et techniques* (Geneva: Médecine et Hygiène, 1974), 20; and L. Bolens, "Agriculture in the Islamic World," in H. Selin (ed.) *Encyclopedia of the History of Science, Technology and Medicine in Non-Western Cultures* (New York: Springer, 1997), 20–22.

[28] D. Fuks, A. Oriya, and E. Weiss, "Innovation or Preservation? Abbasid Aubergines, Archaeobotany, and the Islamic Green Revolution," *Archaeological & Anthropological Sciences* 12.2 (2020): 1–16. On the transmission of agricultural ideas and practices from antiquity, see K. Butzer, "The Islamic Traditions of Agroecology: Crosscultural Experience, Ideas and Innovation," *Ecumene: Journal of Environment, Culture Meaning* 1 (1994): 7–50.

The Land–Water Relationship

A key feature of landscape in the premodern Islamic world is that land and water were generally treated as inseparable. Indeed, the term *wādī*, which in classical Arabic refers to a seasonal stream, in Yemen refers colloquially to both the watercourse and the land it irrigates, reflecting the interdependency of the two elements.[29] The attachment of water to land reflected the social prioritization of agriculture.

In the very first century of Islam in the eastern Mediterranean and the Middle East, when land was typically acquired through conquest, the state owned the agricultural land and granted concessions to farmers to settle and cultivate it. (Land acquired through treaty was more likely to remain in the hands of the vanquished.) Thus, the appropriation of land occurred as a consequence of working the property or building an irrigation canal to make dry land arable. But even then, capital investments alone were not recognized as claims to ownership. For ongoing tenure to be maintained, labor, irrigation, and cultivation were required.[30]

In most areas of the Islamic world, when land was sold, it was conveyed along with the rights to the water that irrigated it. In the Yemeni highlands, where water flowed in very small amounts from mountain springs, the right to the water was transferred when the land was sold or inherited. In some cases, water rights could be temporarily rented out, allowing some degree of flexibility for Yemeni farmers whose needs for water might be greater or lesser according to the crop and the season.[31]

In a few areas of the Islamicate Mediterranean, such as Alicante (eastern Spain), water was treated as a marketable commodity that could be sold.[32] But far more often it was treated as a common good in which case, while it could be used to irrigate fields or turn millstones, it could not be permanently possessed but had to be released to the next persons wishing to water their fields or turn their mills. This principle is at the very core of Islamic ethics, as expressed in the various Hadith on the topic of water. In adjudicating a complaint levied against one Zubayr who was presumably hoarding water on his land, the Prophet was reported to have said: "O Zubayr! Irrigate (your land) first and then let the water flow (to the land of the others)." And in the same Hadith he enjoined the farmer

---

[29] Hehmeyer, *History of Water Engineering*, 80–82.

[30] Wilkinson, "Muslim Land and Water Law." But there is no clear legal policy toward land as property, prompting Perry Anderson to comment that "A pervasive ambiguity and improvisation characteristically haunted landownership in the early centuries of Islam" (*Lineages of the Absolutist State* [London: Verso, 1979], 499).

[31] D. Varisco, "Irrigation in an Arabian Valley: A System of Highland Terraces in the Yemen Arab Republic," *Expedition* 25.2 (1983), 28–29.

[32] T. Glick, *Irrigation and Society in Medieval Valencia* (Cambridge, MA: Harvard University Press, 1970), 13.

to "Irrigate (your land) and withhold the water till it reaches the walls between the pits around the trees," which the Hadith transmitter interpreted as meaning "up to the ankles."[33] This was generally interpreted as an exhortation to use whatever water was reasonably needed for irrigation but to allow the remainder to be used by others.[34] In this sense the water was regarded like air: a necessary resource to be used and shared but not individually possessed.

In this system, whether water fell to earth as rain, was trapped by a dam, or was raised in buckets from a subterranean source, it usually could not be sold except as an attribute of the land it irrigated. In farmland that had been improved by the installation of irrigation canals, it was the increased value of the land (which could now sustain a much greater variety of crops) that raised its market price, not the water itself.[35] In cities where water might be drawn from public wells and carried by a water seller for use in individual households, it was the labor that exacted compensation, not the water. Ibn Khaldun alluded to this principle in his explanation of how profit derives from labor: "Man obtains (some profit) through no efforts of his own, as, for instance, through rain that makes the fields thrive, and similar things. However, these things are only contributory. His own efforts must be combined with them."[36]

This principle that water belongs to the community as a whole is reflected in the water system in the city of Granada, developed from the eleventh through the fifteenth century. Lacking a natural source on the hilltop (which later became known as the Albaicín) where the rulers of the Zirid dynasty (1013–1090) first settled, the Zirid founder's grandson Badis (1038–73) commanded that a canal should be built to carry water across ten kilometers from a mountain source called the Fuente Grande (Figure 9). Although the fabric of that new canal seems to have incorporated some portions of a much older derelict Roman canal (as had occurred in Cordoba),[37] it was nonetheless an enormous, complicated, and costly undertaking that enabled the future growth of the city. The canal – the Acequia de Aynadamar (meaning "canal of the spring of tears") – served three sets of constituents: the farmers in the countryside outside of Granada, the millers who relied on the rapidly flowing water to turn their mills, and above all the city dwellers who needed water for drinking and bathing. An early seventeenth-century diagram shows the canal's diagonal route from the Fuente Grande in the upper left, through the village of Viznar, continuing until it reached the arched

---

[33] Bukhari, *Al-Adab al-Mufrad*, III, Book 40, numbers 548, 549, and 500.
[34] Wilkinson, "Muslim Land and Water Law." See also D. Caponera, *Water Laws in Moslem Countries* (Rome: Food and Agriculture Organization of the United Nations, 1954).
[35] Caponera, *Water Laws*, 39.   [36] Ibn Khaldun, *Muqaddimah*, 297.
[37] A. Orihuela Uzal, and L. J. García Pulido. "El Suministro de agua en la Granada islámica," in *Ars Mechanica* (s.l.: Ministerior de Fomento, CEDEX-CEHOPU, 2008), 144.

Figure 9 The Fuente Grande in Alfacar, Granada (photo: D.F. Ruggles)

portal of the walled city whereupon it divided into multiple branches that flowed from one cistern to the next, represented as boxes (Figure 10).[38]

In this system, one especially large subterranean cistern was housed inside the Zirid palace, from where the king's servants could raise water from a wellhead in the courtyard floor. But there was also an opening on the palace's exterior wall that allowed neighboring residents to lower their buckets into the depths (Figures 11 and 12).[39] In providing water to the public in this way, the king fulfilled the Hadith that reported the Prophet as commending the charity of filling another person's bucket with water.[40] Most of the other cisterns were attached to mosques where the public could get their water from a well in the mosque's courtyard or through an adjacent ablution facility.[41] Today most of the cisterns (all of which still exist) can be found near churches, because the churches were built on the site of the former mosques.

---

[38] A. Orihuela Uzal, and C. Vílchez Vílchez, *Aljibes públicos de la Granada islámica* (Granada: Ayuntamiento de Granada, 1991); Orihuela Uzal and García Pulido, "El Suministro de agua," 144–49.

[39] D. F. Ruggles, "The Aljibe del Rey in Granada," in A. Bigelow (ed.), *Islam through Objects* (London: Bloomsbury, 2021), 73–188.

[40] Bukhari, *Al-Adab al-Mufrad*, no. 304, no. 891, and no. 1182.

[41] Trillo San José, "Entre Rey y la Comunidad: El Agua del Albaizín (Granada) en la Edad Media," *Meridies: Revista de Historia* Medieval 10 (2012): 151–74; Orihuela Uzal and Vílchez Vílchez, *Aljibes públicos de la Granada islámica*.

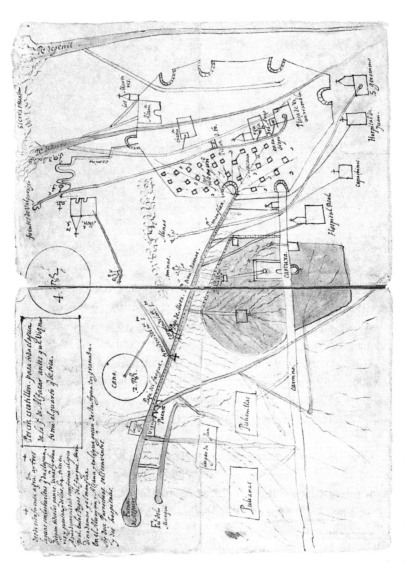

Figure 10 Seventeenth-century diagram of the Aynadamar canal (courtesy: Archivo Histórico de la Facultad de Teología, Granada)

Figure 11 Exterior face of the Aljibe del Rey, Granada (photo: D.F. Ruggles)

Outside of Islamic cities, land that depended on rainfall – dryland – was at the mercy of the weather, which might extend for long periods without precipitation, and thus it was worth much less than land with an irrigation infrastructure in which the flow was steady. Few plants and trees could grow well under dry conditions – the olive and the grape being the notable examples of such crops, but even these produced a better yield when given some water. Unirrigated land was more difficult to cultivate, and therefore more likely to be uncultivated. Moreover, in al-Andalus, dryland that had not been planted for three years could be claimed by anyone, and thus it had less value.[42]

Despite the fact that water was not treated as a commodity, in arid regions the use of water held in common was highly regulated precisely because it had to be shared. This was the case in *wadi* and canal systems where each stakeholder was allowed a certain portion of the water flow. Privately owned wells and water from other private sources did not have to be shared, but these sources generally

---

[42] C. Trillo San José, "Contribución al estudio de la propiedad de la tierra en época nazarí," in C. Trillo San José (ed.), *Asentamientos Rurales y Territorio en el Mediterráneo Medieval* (Granada: Athos-Pérgamos, 2002), 499–535.

Figure 12 Barrel-vaulted interior of the Aljibe del Rey, Granada. Skylights allowed rainwater to enter the cistern during the rainy season (photo: D.F. Ruggles)

yielded less water than that obtained from rivers and large communal canal systems. There were numerous ways that water could be obtained for household use or for agricultural irrigation, each with its own degree of efficiency and rules regarding usage. These systems fall into three main categories: water lifted from below-ground sources, water that flows gravitationally from above-ground sources, and the *qanat*. Each system led to the development of a distinct technology, with different social and economic costs and outcomes.

2 Technology: Water from Below

In the managed landscape of Islam, water "from below" was extracted from wells and rivers, sources that are lower than the surface of the surrounding landscape. To be used for irrigation or in the household, the water had to be lifted up from its source using devices that ranged from the humble bag-and-pulley system and *shaduf* (lever), to more complex waterwheels that could be propelled by a draft animal or powered by running water. Raising water up from below-ground sources was costly for a farmer because every bucketful thus obtained incurred a cost in the labor of a draft animal and often a human operator as well.

Bag and Pulley

One simple way to raise water from a below-ground source was the bag-and-pulley method, which was used since the Assyrian period where it appeared on ninth-century BCE wall reliefs.[43] In the Maghreb the device is known as *sānya* (also *dalw* or *dawlāb*) and in Iraq as *bakra* (Figure 13).[44] It consists of a large, open-mouthed, conical leather bag that can hold 15–35 liters and that is suspended on a rope.[45] The other end of the rope is passed through a pulley or simply thrown over a horizontal axle and then attached to the yoke of a camel, or more likely an ox or donkey, so that as the animal approaches the well or river, the bag drops down into it and fills with water. As the animal walks away from the well (usually on a downward slope so as to add its weight to the overall lifting power), it pulls the bag upward to a point where it spews into a trough. The same method works when a human pulls the ropes. The most efficient version uses two ropes, one attached to the bag's mouth, the other to its tail which serves to upend the bag to decant its contents. The animal or person walks back and forth, endlessly filling and emptying the bag.

The bag-and-pulley system uses no cogwheels or complex machinery (it doesn't even require an actual pulley) and thus does not require sophisticated engineering to install the system. Although its output is low, its benefit to the medieval farmer was that it cost little to install and did not require special environmental conditions for its operation. Moreover, by placing two animals side by side on the track, the same well could yield twice as much. The drawbacks of the bag and pulley were that it required a draft animal – a significant capital investment for a small farmer – and each circuit of the animal yielded only one bag of water.

---

[43] T. J. Wilkinson, and L. Rayne, "Hydraulic Systems in the Middle East," in H. Selin (ed.), *Encyclopaedia of the History of Science, Technology, and Medicine in Non-Western Cultures* (New York: Springer, 2014), pp. 2244-2263.

[44] G. S. Colin, "La noria marocaine et les machines hydrauliques dans le monde árabe," *Hespéris* 4 (1932): 22–60; J. J. Despois, "Bir, iii, the Maghreb," in *The Encyclopaedia of Islam*, 2nd ed. (1960), I: 1231–2; El-Samarraie, *Agriculture in Iraq*, 29.

[45] Despois, "Bir."

Figure 13 Bag-and-pulley system in Metlili, Algeria, in which a camel pulls one bucket and humans pull the other (Photo: Couverchel, *Le Tour du Monde*, 1863/ Alamy)

Due to its simplicity and low cost, the bag and pulley was ubiquitous in most parts of the early Islamic world, from the Maghreb in the west to Yemen and Iraq in the east.[46] However, there are no descriptions of its use in al-Andalus, probably because the Iberian Peninsula, with its ranges of mountains, largely depended on systems of "water from above."

Shaduf

Another mechanism for raising water from below is the *shaduf* (also known as *dāliya* which literally refers to a leather bucket).[47] A relatively primitive form of technology that has been known since 2500 BCE, the *shaduf* is inexpensive to make, requiring only a bucket, some tall poles, rope, and a large stone for counterweight (Figure 14).[48] To build it, a sturdy pole with a fork at its upper end is driven vertically into the ground. A long horizontal pole balances like a seesaw on this fork, which acts as the fulcrum. A stone or some other type of

---

[46] A. Wilson, "Classical Water Technology in the Early Islamic World," 115–41; A. Wilson, D. Mattingly, and M. Sterry, "The Diffusion of Irrigation Technologies in the Sahara in Antiquity," in C. Duckworth, A. Cuénod, and D. Mattingly (eds.), *Mobile Technologies in the Ancient Sahara and beyond* (Cambridge: Cambridge University Press, 2020), 68–114.
[47] Colin, "La noria marocaine," 35.
[48] Wilkinson and Rayne, "Hydraulic Systems in the Middle East."

THE SHADUF.

Figure 14 *Shaduf* in Egypt (Amelia B. Edwards, *A Thousand Miles up the Nile*, 1888)

weight is tied to one end of the horizontal pole to act as a counterweight, while at the other is attached a large water vessel in the form of a wooden bucket or leather bag. Often there is a rope hanging from the end with the vessel so that the operator can grab it and use it to dip the vessel into the source. The operator then swings the pole on its fulcrum, easily moving the water upward and sideways to dump it into a canal or pool. An alternative version uses leather straps to suspend the weighted pole from a horizontal shaft that rests on two uprights, but the mechanism is otherwise the same.

In field observation of modern *shadufs* in Chad, the vessels averaged 15 liters in capacity and could carry about 33 pounds. One *shaduf* could irrigate about one-third of an acre (1,250 square meters).[49] Working as quickly as eight seconds per

---

[49] T. H. Mirti, W.W. Wallender, W.J. Chancellor, and M.E. Grismer, "Performance Characteristics of the Shaduf: A Manual Water-Lifting Device," *Applied Engineering in Agriculture* 15.3 (1999): 225–31. This modest amount is confirmed by other observational studies, but it differs from the description offered in the anonymous eleventh-century *Kitab al-hawi li'l-a'mal*

cycle, a human operator can quickly raise water from a basin, river, or well to the higher ground where it is to be used. Clearly, more height is gained, and thus efficiency improved, with taller vertical poles (but not necessarily longer horizontal poles, which move the water a greater distance but require more time to do so).

The *shaduf* has obvious advantages and disadvantages as a mechanism for lifting water. One drawback is that the work cannot be performed by a draft animal: it requires the dexterity of a human operator. Moreover, the *shaduf* is limited with respect to productivity because, even working at an efficient pace, the water is still moved bucketful by bucketful, such that one device cannot irrigate a very large area. In addition to limited speed, the device is also constrained by height, generally able to lift water not more than two or three meters. This is a limit that can be overcome, however, by organizing the levers in sequence so that the dump basin for one is the source basin for the next, as in the case of the *shaduf* pictured in this nineteenth-century print (see Figure 14).

Perhaps the greatest advantage of the *shaduf* is that it is conceptually simple, comprising inexpensive local materials, and adaptable to environmental conditions. It can be erected just about anywhere but is ideal for riverbanks where it can dip to a greater or lesser depth as needed, adjusting its reach to the seasonally fluctuating water levels of a river. This explains why the *shaduf* was such a popular water-lifting device along the banks of the Nile.

Archimedes Screw

The Archimedes screw, or screw pump, called a *ṭanbūra* (drum), is worth mentioning even though it was not widely used.[50] It consists of a long shaft with a helical wooden blade that is inserted into a large wooden cylinder (often a hollowed-out tree trunk) and made to revolve by means of a paddle or hand crank attached to the central shaft (Figure 15). The lower end draws from the water source, while the upper end discharges the water into the trough that takes it to where it will be used. Although it is named for Archimedes, the great Greek inventor of the third century BCE, historians debate whether or not it was really his innovation. In any case it seems to have been inspired by observing the function of waterwheels that trapped and lifted water in compartments (for which, see further).[51]

---

al-sultaniya wa rusum al-hisab al-diwaniya from Iraq which stated that a *shaduf* with four workers could irrigate 4 *jarib* (5.88 hectares, or 14.53 acres) in winter; 30 (44 hectares, or 109 acres) in summer. See C. Cahen, "Le service de l'irrigation en Iraq au début du XIe siècle," *Bulletin d'études orientales* 13 (1949–51): 117–43.

[50] Colin, "La noria marocaine."

[51] T. Koetsier, and H. Blauwendraat, "The Archimedean Screw-Pump: A Note on Its Invention and the Development of the Theory," in *Proceedings of the International Symposium on History of Machines and Mechanisms* (New York: Springer, 2004), 181–94.

Islamicate Environments

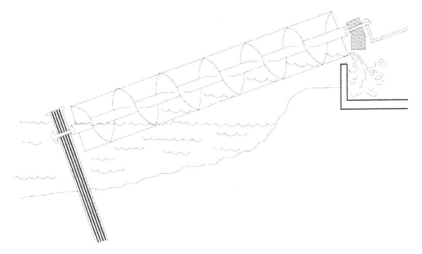

Figure 15 Archimedes screw pump (drawing: B. Variava)

Because the screw pump is fairly small – generally only 2 meters long – it can be moved to different locations and its angle adjusted to suit the context. Thus, its primary advantage is the flexibility of application in any given environment. As the helical blade turns, a generous and continuous flow of water is produced at the upper end of the tube. But because it has to be positioned at an angle, its 2-meter length translates to only a modest rate of actual lift. In most respects, the screw pump is more suitable for removing water, as for example from the bilge of a boat or from marshland, than for lifting it for irrigation. One of the screw pump's other disadvantages is the requirement of a human operator, although in some cases the pump can be propelled by a draft animal. In those more complicated animal-driven machines, the central shaft remains stationary while the outer cylinder is encircled by a flanged wheel that is turned by a cogwheel. Since the cogwheel can be propelled by a yoked draft animal walking in circles, the machine is more efficient.

The device was known to the Romans, as indicated by the thorough explanation of the screw pump given by Vitruvius in the first century BCE.[52] Like the *shaduf*, the screw pump is a good way to lift water from rivers; hence it was used frequently along the banks of the Nile. There is no evidence of its use in al-Andalus, most likely because – as in the case of the bag and pulley – the mountainous terrain provided enough water that only small quantities had to be raised from rivers and wells.

---

[52] Vitruvius, *The Ten Books on Architecture*, trans. M. H. Morgan (Cambridge, MA: Harvard University Press., 1914), Book 10, section vi.

The Waterwheel

Vitruvius also described waterwheels: one type in which water vessels are attached to the rim of the rotating wheel and a tympanum type in which the wheel has internal chambers that fill with water.[53] These were a Roman legacy that was put to wide use in the Islamic environment. In general, Islamic waterwheels can be classified according to (1) those in which ceramic jugs or buckets were attached directly to the wheel (*nāʿūra*, or noria) and (2) those in which the vessels were suspended on a rope (a type often referred to in English as a pot garland, and in Arabic *sāqiya*) (Figure 16). Moreover, wheels can also be divided according to whether they are driven by a draft animal or propelled by the current of a river or canal, and according to whether they have a long or short shaft. The local Arabic terminology is not consistent in the terms used to describe the various types of wheels, and so, to avoid confusion, and because the power source is a key factor in the output of a wheel, I will simply refer to these descriptively as either water-driven or animal-driven wheels, using the term noria (derived from *nāʿūra*) interchangeably with all of them.

Figure 16 Waterwheel with attached ceramic cups, Egypt (Photo: Michele and Tom Grimm/Alamy)

---

[53] Vitruvius, *Ten Books*, Book 10, sections iv and v.

Islamicate Environments

Large and small waterwheels were used across the Islamic world. Al-Muqqadasi observed them in Iran, Ibn Battuta and Yaqut saw them in Syria, Nasir-i Khusrau saw them in Egypt, and Ibn Bassal and al-Idrisi saw them in al-Andalus, and in addition to these textual descriptions, archaeological evidence abounds. As well as wheels used in landscape contexts, numerous diagrams of waterwheels were made in service of what were dubbed "Ingenious Devices," or automata.[54] The earliest manuscript describing automata was a ninth-century Arabic manual called the *Kitab al-hiyal* written by a trio of brothers called the Banu Musa bin Shakir.[55] But the best known was al-Jaziri's *The Book of Ingenious Mechanical Devices*, finished in either 1204 or 1206, divided into six sections on various mechanical topics, accompanied by 173 accurately rendered technical drawings, many of them pertaining to the movement and lifting of water (Figure 17). Section IV of the book is "On the construction in pools of fountains which change their shape, and of machines for the perpetual flute," while section V is "On the construction of machines for raising water from standing water which is not deep, and from a running river." While the illustrations show fanciful contraptions of table-top size, in which water spews from the mouths of lions while miniature oxen and donkeys seem to propel a cogged shaft, the engineering principles were the same as those of larger machines in the working landscape. Indeed, the very operations that were miniaturized in the automaton drawings could also be seen in the actual world: the agricultural landscape must have offered many such scenes of draft animals walking in slow circles to turn a waterwheel.

At the same time, the imaginative way that water was used in the automata to suggest vitality can be seen in palaces such as the Alhambra in Granada, famous for its water basin(s) that rests on the backs of 12 marble lions spewing water (Figure 18). Various fragments of other zoomorphic fountains or vessels have been recovered at other sites such Madinat al-Zahra' and the eleventh-century Qala Bani Hammad palace in the mountains of Algeria.

Waterwheels also appear in narrative scenes in manuscript paintings. A spiral scoop – a variant of the tympanum wheel – is pictured in the *Māqāmat*, a collection of picaresque tales that circulated in the Arabic-

---

[54] A. K. Coomaraswamy, *The Treatise of al-Jazari* (Boston: Museum of Fine Arts, 1924); D. Hill (trans. and ed.), *Ibn al-Razzaz al-Jaziri, The Book of Ingenious Mechanical Devices* (Boston: D. Reidel, 1974).

[55] D. Hill (trans.), Banu Musa bin Shakir, *The Book of Ingenious Devices* (*Kitab al-Hiyal*) (Boston: D. Reidel, 1979); A. Y. al-Hasan (ed.), *Kitab al-Hiyal: The Book of Ingenious Devices* (Aleppo: University of Aleppo, 1981).

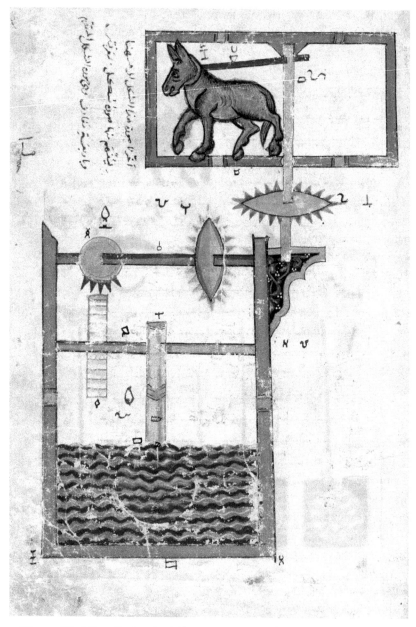

Figure 17 al-Jazari's *Book of Ingenious Mechanical Devices*, illustration painted in 1315 (courtesy: Metropolitan Museum of Art)

speaking world from the eleventh century onward and that was illustrated by al-Wasiti in 1236. One scene shows a musical party assembled at the foot of a fruit tree around a small pool, the water of which is shown to

Figure 18 Lions fountain at the Alhambra Palace, Granada
(photo: D.F. Ruggles)

swirl dynamically (Figure 19). The basin is fed by a water scoop driven by two oxen and a frowning worker behind the stone wall that separates the scene of labor from the scene of leisure.

In the *Bayāḍ wa Riyāḍ*, a thirteenth-century Andalusi story of thwarted love, the waterwheel plays a more dramatic role.[56] In one of the manuscript's images, the heartbroken lover throws himself in despair on the banks of a river, his turban unspooling to suggest his loss of composure, while behind him looms a great noria, a popular poetic symbol (Figure 20). The waterwheel often appeared in poetic metaphors as a melancholic trope: in one the wheel is said to "weep and voice her grief," while in another the waterwheel sings a plaintive love song remembering its first lover. Sometimes the sound was perceived as mellifluous, but some poets and travelers described the endless creaking of the noria as a source of irritation.[57] As a large, dramatic, and spectacularly animated object, the waterwheel had a place in the realm of the

---

[56] A. D'Ottone, "Il manoscritto Vaticano arabo 368, Hadit Bayad wa Riyad. Il codice, il testo, le immagini," *Rivista di Storia della Miniatura* 14 (2010): 55–70; C. Robinson, *Medieval Andalusian Courtly Culture in the Mediterranean: Hadith Bayad wa Riyad* (New York: Routledge, 2007).

[57] Ibn Battuta, *The Travels of Ibn Battuta*, ed. H. A. R. Gibb, 3 vols. (New York, Routledge: 2016), I: 91 on the "screeching" of a waterwheel, and I: 92 on the waterwheel that weeps; on the first lover, Lisan al-Din Ibn Khatib, *A'mal al-A'lam*, in H. Pérès, *Esplendor de al-Andalus: la poesía andaluza en árabe clásico s.XI*, trans. M. García Arenal (Madrid: Hiperión, 1983), 209.

Figure 19 The *Maqamat* of al-Hariri, illustrated in 1237 by al-Wasiti (Paris Bibliotheque Nationale/Alamy Images)

literary and artistic imagination as much as in the utilitarian world of drawing water for irrigation.

The Water-Powered Noria

In agricultural and urban environments, the simplest kind of waterwheel had no gears and consisted of a vertically positioned wheel with tube-like ceramic cups lashed to its rim, or in some variants, wooden compartments. Because the cups could only scoop water that the wheel could reach, the

Figure 20 *Hadith Bayad wa Riyad* (Biblioteca Apostolica Vaticana, MS. ar. 368/Alamy)

wheel's efficacy was limited by its diameter. In this kind of wheel, the river was the source for water as well as the source for power to rotate the device. In more elaborate arrangements, the river propelled one wheel with paddles along its rim instead of ceramic cups, which in turn caused a second wheel to rotate. Taking advantage of the river current in this way removed the primary cost of running a waterwheel, which was labor. Propelled by the river and without the need for a draft animal, such a wheel could operate all day and night, lifting a steady supply of water from the river up to the land above.

In his study of ninth-century Iraq, Husam Qawam El-Samarraie wrote that a standard water-powered waterwheel had 8 cups attached to it, each of which carried 15 *ratl*s of water and made 250 turns per hour. (The *ratl* was a measure of volume that varied considerably according to geographic area and the material being weighed.)[58] Thus, when running at full capacity, one waterwheel could provide irrigation for 1,592 square meters of land (not quite half an acre). But when the river's level was lower and its current slower, as in the summer months, it produced much less.[59] On the Orontes River in Syria, where the wheels were much larger and encircled by a great many more noria cups, water was raised at an average rate of 45 liters per second and irrigated 25 hectares (61.77 acres) of land. In the largest wheel – twenty-one meters in diameter – which is dated by inscription to 1362, the rate of lift was 150–180 liters per second, irrigating up to 75 hectares (185 acres).[60] Some thirty-two enormous wheels stood on the banks of the Orontes River, and in Hama, fifteen of these survived at least until the late 1980s. Many of the wheels of Hama were funded through the strategy of *waqf*, a religious endowment in which the *waqf* register typically also named the gardens, fields and buildings that were served by the waterwheel. This was surely the case for the Noria al-Muḥammadiyya which served the congregational mosque. Its inscription reads: "This big and blessed water-wheel was constructed to carry water to the al-Aʻlā Mosque in the days of our Lord, His Most Noble Excellency Saif al-dīn Ṭānyaraqi, Viceroy of the province of Ḥamā, during the last days of the year 763 (1362)."[61] Other wheels were the work of elite patrons, such as the Noria al-Maʻmūriyya which had an inscription giving the name of its founder, the emir of Hama, and the date June 1453.[62]

The waterwheels of Hama were powered by the river's current, which was intensified as it rushed through the low weirs built across the river's width. The wheels, which stood on both sides of the river, raised the water and delivered it via aqueducts to the main irrigation canal from which it flowed downhill via secondary canals (Figure 21). In the fourteenth century the city and its waterwheels were admired by Ibn Battuta who found Hama "of exceeding comeliness and surpassing beauty, and surrounded by orchards and gardens, supplied by water-wheels like celestial globes."[63] The surviving wheels are of the tympanum type (called *tābūt* or *dawlāb*) – a variety in use since the Roman period – in which water is scooped up in wedge-shaped compartments, or drums, along the wheel's rim. The

---

[58] E. Ashtor, "Levantine Weights and Standard Parcels: A Contribution to the Metrology of the Later Middle Ages," *Bulletin of the School of Oriental and African Studies* 45.3 (1982): 471–88.

[59] El-Samarraie, *Agriculture in Iraq*, 25–30.

[60] A. de Miranda, *Water Architecture in the Lands of Syria: The Water-Wheels* (Rome: 'L'Erma' di Bretschneider, 2007), 100–3, 123–24.

[61] De Miranda, *Water Architecture*, 123–4.

[62] A. R. Zaqzouq, "Les Norias: anciens moyens d'Irrigation les Plus Importants dans la Région de Hama," in *Techniques et Pratiques Hydro-Agricoles Traditionelles en Domaine Irrigué (Actes de Colloque de Damas, 27 juin -1 juillet 1987)* 2 vols. (Paris: Librarie Orientaliste Paul Geunther, 1990), II: 337–65.

[63] Adapted from Ibn Battuta, *Travels*, I: 91.

Figure 21 Waterwheels on the Orontes River in Hama (photo: Franco Pecchio/ Creative Commons)

water thus trapped is released when the compartment reaches the top of the wheel's circuit, pouring out through an opening in the side of the drum.[64]

In Cordoba, the waterwheels that stretched across the width of the Guadalquivir River on the downstream (western) side of the great Roman bridge powered mills. Thus positioned, they took full advantage of the acceleration in the river's current as it pushed through the bridge's arched openings. Just outside the city walls, and near the congregational mosque, there was a particularly enormous wheel that lifted water up to the governor's palace on the river's northern bank (Figure 22). According to an unpublished Arabic manuscript read by the historian Levi-Provençal, the waterwheel – known as the Albolafia – was built c. 1136–1137 by the Almoravid governor of Cordoba, Yusuf ibn Tashfin. Support for this attribution is given by al-Maqqari, writing in the early seventeenth century, who referred to an Almohad-era wheel.[65] While the stone foundations have been preserved, the current wooden wheel is a replacement made in 1965.[66] In the thirteenth century when one observer

---

[64] Oleson, *Greek and Roman Mechanical Water-Lifting Devices*, 9–10.
[65] L. Torres Balbás, "La Albolafia de Córdoba y la gran noria toledana," *Al-Andalus* 7 (1942): 175–83.
[66] F. Hernández Giménez, "Restauración en el molino de la Albolafia de Córdoba," *Al-Mulk* 2 (1961–1962): 161–73.

Figure 22 Aboulafia waterwheel and bridge at Cordoba (photo: Daniel Martín Trani/Alamy)

described 5,000 waterwheels along the Guadalquivir River, these were most likely mills for grinding the grain grown in the area.[67]

In fact, any water artery with a sufficient rate of flow would have offered a prime opportunity for watermills, for which reason even a large canal could drive a mill. Granada's Acequia de Aynadamar, powered numerous mills in the eleventh century and later.

Animal-powered Noria

Unlike the water-powered wheel, the animal-driven wheel had to have gears. The one exception was the treadwheel operated by a human being, in which steps were attached to the wheel's rim so that a person could turn the wheel by "walking" up it. But this does not seem to have been a popular type of noria. The geared wheel – actually two cogwheels intermeshed – was of Roman origin and was described by Vitruvius.[68] The geared wheel was most likely to be used with a loop of vessels suspended from the wheel's rim. (It is important to remember that there are multiple groups to which any wheel might belong: (1) water- or (2) animal-powered wheels, and (3) wheels to which the vessels are attached directly to the rim or (4) wheels with the pots suspended from

---

[67] Al-Maqqari, *History of the Mohammedan Dynasties in Spain*, ed. and trans. P. de Gayangos, 2 vols. (London: Oriental Translation Fund, 1840–3), I: 41–42, citing al-Shaqundi.
[68] Vitruvius, *Ten Books*, Book 10, chapter 5.

Islamicate Environments

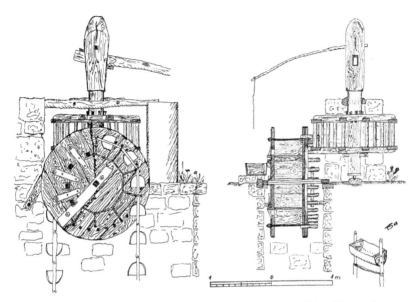

Figure 23 Waterwheel view and section (drawing: Thorkild Schiøler, *Roman and Islamic Water-Lifting Wheels*)

a looped rope. With these four variables, different types of wheels were made.) Because the animal-driven wheel does not require a river to provide power, it could be used anywhere. It was ideal for houses and small gardens where water had to be lifted from a well, and this is how it seems to have been employed in the Roman era. But in the Islamic era, such devices were more widely applied. In this type of wheel, a draft animal was yoked to a long horizontal bar which, as the animal walked in circles, rotated a horizontal cogwheel (Figure 23). The noria pictured here meshed with the cogs of a vertical wheel that was set above the water source. Instead of lashing the vessels to the vertical wheel, as would be the case in the water-powered wheel, they were attached to a long rope looped around the rim and in this way the vessels could be dipped into a water source below ground, reaching far below waterwheel's diameter. As the vessels tilt at the highest point, the water splashes into a basin or canal. Because of the gear mechanism, this was a sophisticated and presumably expensive machine but it was also more dangerous: Thorkild Schiøler's description of the water-powered wheel mentions the importance of a brake mechanism (called a pawl) that prevents the wheel from going into reverse and dragging the yoked draft animal.[69]

---

[69] T. Schiøler, *Roman and Islamic Water-Lifting Wheels* (Denmark: Odense University Press, 1971), 20; D. Hill, *A History of Engineering in Classical and Medieval Times* (London: Croom Hill, 1984), 136–7.

The drawbacks of this kind of animal-propelled waterwheel are that it was a permanent installation that could not easily be moved, and it required animal labor. The system, which does not require proximity to a river, is ideal for lifting water from a deep but confined source, such as a cistern, because it can reach great depths. Historically it was also used in architectural environments for raising water to elevated heights in multi-storied houses and hilltop fortresses. Its greatest advantage was that its capacity to lift water was limited only by the length of the looped rope. The Persian traveler Nasir-i Khusraw, visiting Fustat (Cairo) in the mid-eleventh century, observed how waterwheels made it possible to grow large gardens on the rooftops of houses:

> In the midst of the houses in the city are gardens and orchards watered by wells. In the sultan's harem are the most beautiful gardens imaginable. Waterwheels have been constructed to irrigate them. There are trees planted and pleasure parks built even on the roofs.
>
> I heard from a reliable source that one person has on top of a seven-story house a garden where he raised a calf. He also has a waterwheel up there turned by this ox to lift water from a well down below. He has orange trees and also bananas and other fruit-bearing trees, flowers, and herbs planted on the roof.[70]

In the agricultural landscape, topography determined which type of wheel was best suited for a given environment. The ideal was a river location in which the river flowed steadily without significant fluctuations in level, the flow itself providing the propulsion. Where water had to be raised from subterranean sources, the bucket and chain (pot garland) wheel, was most effective. In arid areas there was reciprocity in that, on the one hand, the land needed water to irrigate its crops, while on the other hand, the design of that same water system was adapted to the preexisting conditions of the land.

Water that must be raised from ground sources, such as wells and rivers, requires investment in machines and incurs a regular operating cost in the form of human or animal labor. Once raised to the level of the farmland, it is delivered via canals; however, at that point, because the water begins to flow gravitationally, it has become "water from above." Because such water is derived from a shared source such as a *wadi*, rather than a well on the landowner's property, a system of regulation is required to ensure fair distribution. Thus, not only the engineering is different, but also the social structure that guides it.

---

[70] Nasir-i Khusraw, *Nasir-i Khusraw's Book of Travels (Safarnama)*, ed. and trans. W. Thackston (Costa Mesa: Mazda, 2001), 60 and 67.

3 Technology: Water from Above

The amount of water yielded by a water-lifting device – even a rapidly rotating noria – is generally much less than the water delivered from a mountain spring or a constructed canal system because one mode of delivery produces water by the bucketful while the other spews a constant stream. Whereas animal- and human-powered water-lifting devices are not operated at night, water that flows down from an elevated source such as rainfall and mountain springs tends to flow constantly (or at least seasonally) for twenty-four hours daily. And because it comprises a network for delivery that crosses between and through the lands of numerous individual proprietors, it compels the various users to form a community and to be guided by a social contract, whether formalized as law or simply a habitual practice. Moreover, as we have seen, the need to control water that falls as rain or flows in a seasonal stream can lead human cultivators to alter the form of the land. For this and other reasons, systems of water catchment from above constitute a hydraulic strategy that differs in significant ways from systems of water from below. The types of water that flow from above that will be considered here are river inundations, the *wadi* (seasonal stream), and the open surface canal.

River Floods

While we may think of a river as a below-ground source that can only be reached with a *shaduf* or noria, in the case of a river that is prone to seasonal flooding, the water runs between elevated banks during periods of low flow but becomes an above-ground source during the period of peak flooding when the river overruns its banks. The Euphrates and Tigris rivers in Iraq and Syria and the Nile in Egypt were prone to seasonal overflows, which – aside from the very real danger of uncontrollable floods – meant that farmers could take advantage of the high-water levels to trap irrigation water for use after the river had receded. The Euphrates and Tigris were frequently subject to erratic seasonal floods, the result of irregular levels of rainfall that brought water but also destruction, especially during the winter months. Moreover, the course of the rivers often wandered. In contrast, the Nile was far more predictable.

The Nile is an enormous river, fed by the White Nile, the Atbara, and the Blue Nile, with origins in East Africa, primarily Ethiopia. The Nile and its tributaries carry a seasonal surge caused by the monsoons that fall on Ethiopia, which has a dramatic effect on the downstream regions where the river overflows its banks. Because Egypt receives virtually no precipitation, it is dependent on the Nile for its water. For much of its history – until the Aswan Dam was completed in 1970 – the Nile's annual inundation was a joyful and much-anticipated event in Cairo because the entire economy and well-being of the people depended on it. The precise level to which the river would rise was not calculable in advance, since that was dependent on annual climatic factors in Ethiopia, but once the river had swelled, its volume was measured and the harvest could be predicted. This information was critical for farmers whose sole source of water was from the river, and it was also important for taxation because agricultural taxes were not levied until the Nile had risen to a sufficient level to allow irrigation. The tight link between water levels and agricultural production is an example of the inseparability of water and land.

In Pharaonic and Roman Egypt, nilometers of various types were built to measure the river's height. Some of them, such as those at Aswan and Dendera, continued in use after the Islamic conquest in the seventh century and were either repaired or replaced by that new set of patrons. Regardless of the political regime, life that was dependent on the Nile's inundations required the maintenance and construction of nilometers. Many of them were little more than open tanks with water level markings recorded on one wall. In contrast to those modest devices, the Cairo Nilometer (*Miqyās al-Nīl*) stands out as a majestic structure, albeit largely hidden below ground. Built at the site of an earlier nilometer, the Cairo Nilometer was constructed in 861 (and restored in 873) on the Rawdah Island in Cairo, and it survives in excellent condition today (Figure 24). Its foundation inscription, which provides the date and names both the designer and the patron, states that in the year it was built "the water level reached seventeen cubits and eighteen fingers."[71] The structure consists of a deep well that reaches down to the level of the Nile water, with a stairway wrapping around the interior. As the Nile rises, river water enters the well through three tunnels. In the center stands a graduated octagonal marble pillar, 10.50 m in height, on the sides of which are marked the water-level measurements.

The Cairo Nilometer has the distinction of being the oldest surviving Islamic monument in Egypt, and it also has the oldest surviving Arabic architectural inscriptions in Egypt. Those include a foundation inscription praising the patron, and several blessings, but the remainder contain Quranic verses, many of which, not surprisingly, pertain to water. Among them:

> 32: 27 (Sūrat al-Sajda)
> Have they not seen that We drive the water to barren land and bring forth thereby crops from which their livestock eat and [they] themselves? Then do they not see?

---

[71] B. O'Kane, *The Monumental Inscriptions of Historic Cairo*. https://islamicinscriptions.cultnat.org/About.html.

Islamicate Environments

Figure 24 The Nilometer of Cairo (photo: D.F. Ruggles)

42:28 (Sūrat al-Shūrā)
And it is He who sends down the rain after they had despaired and spreads His mercy. And He is the Protector, the Praiseworthy.[72]

Given that the letters of the inscription were formerly easily legible against a blue background of lapis lazuli, it is quite likely that the invocations were meant to be read aloud, especially in conjunction with the prayers for optimal flood levels held at various mosques in the city.[73]

As it flowed past Cairo, the river was at its lowest toward the end of May but began to rise around June 10 and reached its peak level in early October. (In Aswan to the south, these phenomena occurred a couple of weeks earlier.) The anxiety about its rise was such that a town crier would publicly call out the level of the flood from the time that it reached 12 cubits until it reached 16 cubits, or about 30 feet, which was the optimal level.[74] Curiously, the Nile flooded later than rivers in most other areas of the Mediterranean because it does not get its water from snowmelt, but rather from the spring and summer monsoon rains in Ethiopia. Thus, whereas Mediterranean agriculture more typically takes

---

[72] O'Kane, *Monumental Inscriptions*.
[73] H. Mostafa, "The Nile as Nexus: The Nilometer at al-Rawda Island between Veneration and Mediation in Medieval Islamic Egypt," in K. Blouin (ed.), *The Nile Delta: Histories from Antiquity to the Modern Period* (Cambridge: Cambridge University Press, 2014), 421–52.
[74] Mostafa, "The Nile as Nexus."

advantage of the cool winter and spring moisture, Egypt does not begin its growing season until the fall when the earth is already baked by the harsh sun.[75]

Before the waters rose, the canal beds had to be dredged and their temporary dams repaired. When the Nile waters began to flood, the protective dams that blocked the canals were opened, allowing the inundation of the flat agricultural land on either side of the river. Some of these were relatively short canals that served the immediate agricultural areas, but others were more significant. The Bahr Yusuf canal (indicated as Bahr Youssef on the map) ran 25 kilometers out into the desert to the huge Fayyum oasis southwest of Cairo (indicated as Medinat-al-Fayoum on the map) (Figure 25).

Upon reaching the oasis, the Bahr Yusuf branched out into fifty-eight smaller canals that led to farms.[76] The water flow in peak season was generous enough that boats could sail into the Fayyum.[77] The Fayyum's al-Lahun dam, which dates from the pharaonic period (like the Bahr Yusuf), kept the water on site, so that, even when the canal stopped delivering water from the Nile, irrigation was possible not just seasonally but all year round, enabling crops such as rice, cotton and sugar cane that demanded a lot of water for their cultivation.[78] This was especially important at the Fayyum because, unlike other oases that were watered by local springs, the Fayyum was entirely dependent on water from the Nile. In a community so dependent on the success of its canal system and dam, one might expect the government to play a key supervising role, but according to al-Nabulusi, a government official who made a detailed description of the region on the occasion of a visit in 1244–45, oversight was achieved by locals: "a large group of men from the villages of al-Fayyum, as well as engineers, [who] gather together." Moreover, he reported that in the preceding century, the Ayyubid administration in Cairo had provided no funds for the Fayyum's irrigation canals, another sign that the system was locally managed and controlled.[79]

Along the Nile, canals carried silt-rich water to fill sunken plots formed by low earthen walls, each plot or basin slightly lower than the one preceding (Figure 26).[80] The silt contained nutrients, yet its buildup was a problem that

---

[75] In the modern era, the Aswan Dam has prevented flooding, causing the buildup of ground salts which has caused the deterioration of architectural foundations throughout Cairo.
[76] T. Sato, "Irrigation in Rural Egypt from the 12th to the 14th Centuries," *Orient* 8 (1972): 81–92.
[77] Y. Rapoport and I. Shahar, "Irrigation in the Medieval Islamic Fayoum: Local Control in a Large-Scale Hydraulic System," *Journal of the Economic and Social History of the Orient* 55 (2012): 1–31.
[78] Sato, "Irrigation in Rural Egypt," and Rapoport and Shahar, "Irrigation in the Medieval Islamic Fayoum," explain that the dam in various periods had a spillway, sluices, and culverts.
[79] Rapoport and Shahar, "Irrigation in the Medieval Islamic Fayoum," 9, citing al-Nabulusi, *Ta'rikh al-Fayyum wa-biladihi*, ed. B. Moritz (Cairo: Publications de la Bibliotheque Khediviale. 1898), 3 and 12.
[80] S. J. Borsch. "Nile Floods and the Irrigation System in Fifteenth-Century Egypt," *Mamluk Studies Review* 4 (2000): 131–45. The diagram shown here is adapted from Borsch.

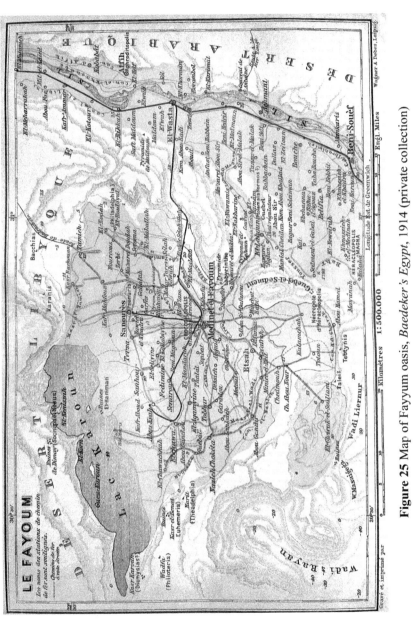

Figure 25 Map of Fayyum oasis, *Baedeker's Egypt*, 1914 (private collection)

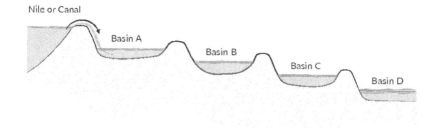

Figure 26 Sequence of flood irrigation basins along the Nile
(drawing: M. Mallula)

required that the canals be cleaned annually. After the water had soaked deep into the soil and begun to recede, seeds could be sowed in the mud. Of course, with the aid of a *shaduf* or waterwheel, plots bordering the river had access to water at other times of the year, but the rest of the riparian landscape relied on the river's inundation. (However, in the Fayyum in the thirteenth century, waterwheels upstream extracted so much water from the canal serving the oasis that the flow was reduced. Thus, the two methods of supplying water were sometimes in conflict.[81])

In good years, the Nile flood was celebrated with the festival of Fath al-Khalij ("opening of the canal"). In the years when the river did not flood enough, there was widespread famine, and in the years when it flooded too much, the fields could not be plowed, catastrophes that the people tried to ward off through prayer and ritual performances. Heba Mostafa's recent study shows the ways that both religion and statecraft were tightly connected to the hydraulic cycle, tracing "the veneration of the Nile not only as the guarantor of Egypt's prosperity, but also as the conduit of divine grace and God's agent of reward and punishment."[82]

The *Wadi*

The irrigation system of the Nile was perfectly suited for its riparian environment. But in more mountainous terrain, water came from rainfall and snowmelt, flowing downward in a sporadic stream called a *wadi*. The simplest way to capture and store the water delivered by *wadi* was a reservoir. Outside of Kairouan, there survive two enormous polygonal water basins, completed in 862–63 in the period of Aghlabid rule, which

---

[81] Rapoport and Shahar, "Irrigation in the Medieval Islamic Fayoum," 9–10, citing al-Nabulusi, *Ta'rikh*, 11–12.
[82] Mostafa, "The Nile as Nexus," 448.

were part of a larger system of hydraulic supply (Figure 27). Receiving water from a *wadi*, they each connect to smaller basins that served as sedimentation tanks that allowed the particulates carried by the water to settle. From there, the water would flow into the larger basin which was 8 meters deep and had an internal diameter of 130 meters.[83] When the water accumulation exceeded the capacity of the two basins, it could be stored in underground barrel-vaulted cisterns located nearby. In his studies of Yemen, Daniel Varisco noted that cisterns were often used nocturnally to store the water that flowed into an agricultural area during the night, allowing an easier and more controlled distribution in the daylight.[84]

In other agricultural areas, a *wadi*'s water went straight to the field for irrigation. *Wadi*s run especially abundantly after a rainfall, but since rain falling on very dry, hard ground will run quickly over it, forming a ravine in which there is erosion but no percolation into the soil, measures must be taken to slow the water's speed and distribute it as widely as possible. This is accomplished by erecting a dam (usually temporary) across the width of the *wadi*. The dam's purpose is not to collect and store water – the excess of which, in times of flooding, can actually pose a threat – but to direct it to the plots of land along its course which are then irrigated by inundation. Human intervention is required to capture and direct the water, but as is typical of "water from above" systems, the investment is one of construction and maintenance, not daily operation. Because *wadi*s capture seasonal precipitation and do not typically flow all year round, their primary goal is to extend the length of time that irrigation can occur.

Qasr al-Hayr East (built 728) is an example of a remote agricultural and trading settlement, the survival and prosperity of which was entirely dependent on the water from a *wadi*. Built in the Syrian desert northeast of Palmyra, the eight-century site included a large walled residence for multiple families as well as a smaller structure for residents or visiting traders, a bathhouse (possibly with an attached reception hall), and cisterns (Figure 28). Encircling this cluster of buildings was an immense, irregularly shaped enclosure made of low mudbrick walls. The presence of olive pits that the archaeologists discovered outside of a processing room in the large residence provided evidence for the type of trees grown within the enclosure. Although olive trees tolerate aridity well, water is needed when the saplings (usually started from cuttings) are first planted, an activity that must have been undertaken opportunistically in the rare times when the water was in sufficient supply. Additionally, the occasional ephemeral flow

---

[83] A.Y. al-Hassan, and D. R. Hill, *Islamic Technology: An Illustrated History* (Cambridge: Cambridge University Press, 1986), 87.

[84] Varisco, "Irrigation in an Arabian Valley," 28.

Figure 27 The Aghlabid basins at Kairouan (photo: Bernard Gagnon/Creative Commons)

from the *wadi* may have been enough for an additional short season crop to be grown in the shade of the trees.[85]

The precise way that Qasr al-Hayr was supplied by water is not entirely clear. There was an underground *qanat* that ran below the *wadi*, so that the *wadi* may have recharged the *qanat*.[86] In rare seasons when rain fell, the *wadi* guided its water toward the entrance at the north end of the enclosure, where the elevation was slightly higher and where a barrier separated the water's influx from the buildings clustered there. It filled the cisterns and flooded the enclosed land, and any excess could then flow out through sluices at the southern and lower end. When the rain fell in that desert environment, it came in torrents that washed quickly over the hard-packed earth, but by containing the water within the enclosure walls so that it could soak more slowly into the earth, more effective irrigation was possible at Qasr al-Hayr East.

Using the methods of ethnohistory to illuminate historic irrigation practices, Ingrid Hehmeyer has studied the way that irrigation by *wadi* occurs in the agricultural area around the western Yemeni city of Zabid, which has the largest *wadi* system in Yemen (Figure 29). Zabid stands on a coastal plain below a range of mountains reaching 3000 meters in altitude on the western edge of Yemen, which is the source for the *wadis*. Zabid has annual and quite variable precipitation that fills the *wadis* in the spring and late summer.[87] To redirect the course of the water that flows into such a stream, a simple temporary dam is typically thrown across its path (although the Wadi Zabid itself was too wide for

---

[85] O. Grabar, R. Holod, J. Knustad, and W. Trousdale, *City in the Desert: Qasr al-Hayr East* (Cambridge, MA: Harvard University Press, 1978), esp. 73–9.
[86] O. Grabar, R. Holod, J. Knustad, and W. Trousdale, *City in the Desert*, 107.
[87] I. Hehmeyer, "Physical Evidence of Engineered Water Systems in Medieval Zabid," *Proceedings of the Seminar for Arabian Studies* (Papers from at the Twenty-Eighth Meeting of the Seminar for Arabian Studies held at Oxford, July 21–23, 1994) 25 (1995): 45–54.

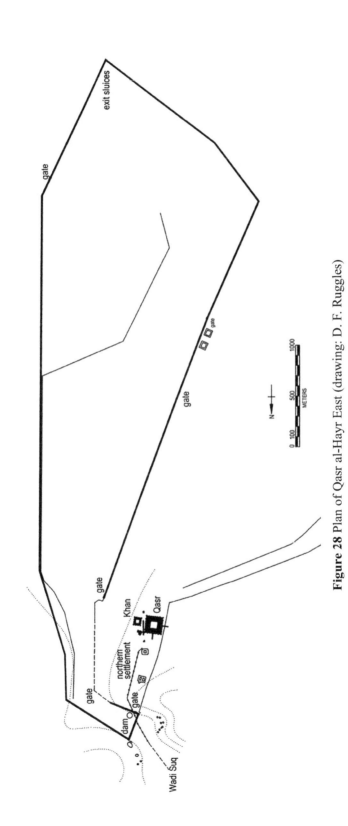

Figure 28 Plan of Qasr al-Hayr East (drawing: D. F. Ruggles)

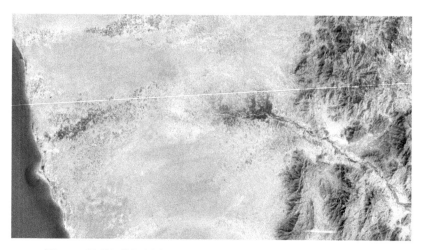

Figure 29 Wadi Zabid, Yemen, aerial image (Google Earth Pro)

such a barrier). This diverts both the water and the rich sediment that it carries into the farmlands flanking the stream. Thus, irrigation is achieved – as in Qasr al-Hayr's enclosure – by the temporary flooding of plots that are defined by low earthen walls. The plots at the head of the *wadi* are inundated first, and then the rest of the plots are flooded in sequence.[88]

Because the water naturally flows downward, each field must be slightly lower than the one from which it receives water, resulting in terracing (see Figure 4). Moreover, as water-borne sediment settles into the walled plot, the soil is enriched and the floor level of the terraces rises over time.[89] In that environment, the land has been reshaped both for and by the management of water.

That this system is a continuation of medieval practices is confirmed by a late thirteenth-century tax register that contains a description and diagram of the Wadi Zabid (Figure 30).[90] Because the spillway was already quite wide, no dam was needed to trap the water in this instance. Instead canals were dug to draw water from the *wadi* and distribute it to the shareholders who belonged to the irrigation network. The diagram shows clearly the spatialization of the water system. East is placed at the top – where the watercourse originates – and west at the bottom – from where it flowed 45 kilometers to the Red Sea. Extending from

---

[88] I. Hehmeyer, *A History of Water Engineering and Management in Yemen* (Leiden: Brill, 2019), esp. 84.

[89] Hehmeyer, *A History of Water Engineering*, 72.

[90] Hehmeyer, *A History of Water Engineering*, 78, citing M. A. Jazim (ed.), *Irtifaʿ al-dawla al-Muʾayyadiyya: Jibayat bilad al-yaman* (Sanʿaʾ: Centre français d'archéologie et de sciences sociales, Deutsches Archaologisches Institut, Sanaa branch, 2008).

Islamicate Environments 49

Figure 30 Zabid tax register diagram (courtesy: Centre français d'archéologie et de sciences sociales, Sanaa branch)

the main watercourse, the diagonal lines represent the canals that supplied the lands that received the water: five canals on the *wadi*'s south bank and twelve canals on the north bank.

As pointed out earlier, the inseparability of land and water means that the term *wadi* in the Yemeni context refers both to the watercourse and the land it feeds, because without the *wadi*'s water, the land would be useless.

Canals

Whether the water was obtained from a naturally flooding river, or by a seasonal *wadi*, it then had to be transported to the point of consumption via canal. These could be canals that ran at a very small rate of decline across a relatively flat landscape, as occurred in Cairo and its surrounding area. Or they could be elaborate systems that had to adapt to a topographically varied terrain and thus demanded careful planning. In many areas of the Mediterranean, surviving Roman canals and aqueducts were reused by Muslim communities, generally so as to incorporate them into a more comprehensive system.

Cordoba's principal palace was Madinat al-Zahra' (completed in 936), an enormous palatine city built for the Umayyad caliph 'Abd al-Rahman III (r. 912–961) about eight kilometers from Cordoba (Figure 31, see also Figure 5). Its emplacement on the lower slope of the Sierra Morena prompted its architects to organize the space in three stepped terraces, with the caliphal quarters at the highest point, ceremonial halls on the middle level, and the orchards, services, and housing for palace staff situated on lower ground. The palace was fed by rainwater that ran down from the low mountains in canals, some of which had been created by the Romans 600 years earlier to serve Roman Corduba (see Figure 3).[91] Thus the palace took advantage of both the natural hydraulic potential of the mountain and the pre-existing waterworks. The water irrigated the palace's gardens and orchards, and it filled the huge fishponds (a source of food for the palace), the moat surrounding the zoo, and the ornamental pools in the palatial quarters. It was also used in bathhouses, and even the latrines where waste was flushed away by water than ran below the pavements (Figure 32). Coursing down from the hills, the water built up enough pressure to cause it to pour from the mouths of zoomorphic fountains, animating them for a dramatic effect that in the medieval world must have elicited amazement.[92]

---

[91] A. Ventura Villanueva, *El abastecimiento de agua a la Córdoba romana. I. El Acueducto de Valdepuentes* (Cordoba: Universidad de Córdoba,1993); D. F. Ruggles, "The Countryside: The Roman Agricultural and Hydraulic Legacy of the Islamic Mediterranean," in S. K. Jayyusi, R. Holod, A. Petruccioli, and A. Raymond (eds.), *The City in the Islamic World*, 2 vols. (Leiden: Brill, 2008), II: 795–815.

[92] Ruggles, *Gardens, Landscape, and Vision*, 81–5.

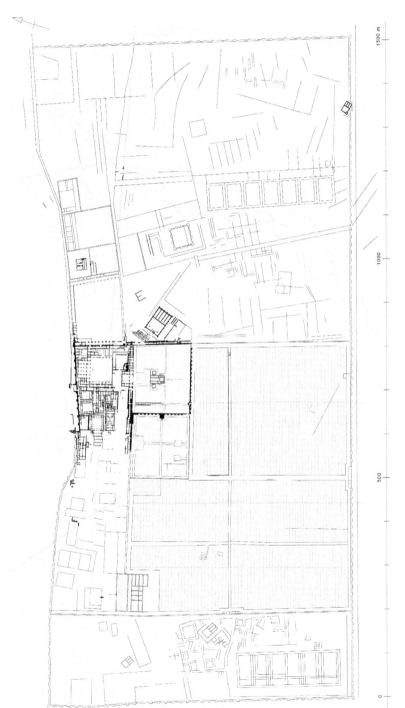

Figure 31 Madinat al-Zahrāʾ (Plan: Felix Arnold/German Archaeological Institute)

Figure 32 Latrine at Madinat al-Zahra' (photo: D.F. Ruggles)

Madinat al-Zahra' was clearly a fiat construction, built at the caliph's command, and yet the selection of its site had necessitated a careful reading of what the environment had to offer. The farmers and owners of *munya*s (agricultural estates) in the river valley at the foot of the palace and outside the walls of Cordoba were already using the natural runoff to irrigate their land, as had the Romans before them. The Roman canals have been traced by archaeologists, and remnants of that system can still be seen along Cordoba's western wall. The fact that such large portions of the Roman hydraulic system were reused by the Muslim rulers demonstrates that water infrastructure and management that are well suited for a given environment are likely to survive, regardless of political and cultural shifts. This is because the conditions that guide the installation of a hydraulic system are first and foremost environmental, in which the deciding factors are the availability of springs, rainfall, topography, slope, and soil type – not the politics of the state. As Miquel Barceló pointed out with regard to his extensive excavations in medieval Mallorca and eastern Spain, irrigation systems work when the environmental conditions are right for them.[93]

---

[93] M. Barceló, "The Design of Irrigation Systems in al-Andalus: A Statement of General Principles," in M. Barceló, H. Kirchner, R. Martí, and J. M. Torres (eds.), *The Design of Irrigation Systems in al-Andalus* (Barcelona: Departament d'Historia et les Societats Precapitalistes i d'Antropologia Social, Universitat Autònoma de Barcelona, 1998), 9–22.

A key question that arises with respect to largescale hydraulic systems such as that of Cordoba is whether they were (1) created all at once as a complete system at the behest of the ruling political authority (a top down and coherent model), (2) formed incrementally, one farmstead and one canal at a time (a bottom up but incoherent model), or (3) designed by local authority (a bottom up and coherent model). The canals of Cordoba were clearly designed to fit the particular environmental niche in which they operated, indicating that the system was coherent. And the impetus for the system came from the caliph himself, as the chronicles of the period attest.

But the case of Madinat al-Zahra' complicates these models because the fact that there was already an underlying Roman system which 'Abd al-Rahman's engineers drew upon for the new canal suggests that this was a matter of environmental opportunism, rather than top-down state planning, even though it was the caliph himself who was the patron. This is not to dismiss the importance of 'Abd al-Rahman's motivations for his patronage. The political impetus for the project was his reclaiming of caliphal titulature a few years earlier in 929, and to finance the new palace city he used one third of the revenues of his kingdom.[94] Moreover, all of the accounts about how water was brought to supply the palace, and all the accounts about how water was brought to supply the ablution facility in the Mosque of Cordoba and irrigate the trees in its courtyard state that the canals were excavated at the ruler's command.[95] Yet this was not a case of untrammeled top-down power, for the canals were public projects that ultimately benefitted everyone. Of key importance, the balance between public duty and royal self-aggrandizement was kept in check: at a moment when the caliph had become so engrossed in the construction of his new palace that he missed the congregation prayers in Cordoba for three weeks in a row, he was publicly rebuked by one of the city's judges.[96] His first duty was to the community as the "commander of the faithful."

In this light, it is best to characterize the hydraulic infrastructure of Cordoba as modelled on the example of ordinary agricultural practice, availing itself of Roman structure to the extent possible, but then extended by the caliph's

---

[94] Ruggles, *Gardens, Landscape, and Vision*, 60, citing Ibn Ghalib, "La descripción de Córdoba de Ibn Galib," trans. J. Vallvé Bermejo, in *Homenaje a Pedro Sáinz Rodríguez*, 4 vols. (Madrid: Fundación Universitaria Española, 1986), III: 674.

[95] D. F. Ruggles, "From the Heavens and Hills: The Flow of Water to the Fruited Trees and Ablution Fountains in the Great Mosque of Cordoba," in S. Blair and J. Bloom (eds.), *Rivers of Paradise: Water in Islamic Art* (London: Yale University Press, 2009), 81–103.

[96] Ruggles, *Gardens, Landscape, and Vision*, 60, citing al-Maqqari, *Analectes*, I: 375.

engineers. (Something similar may have occurred in Granada, where the Acequia de Aynadamar, a long canal bringing water to the Zirid king's hilltop palace, seems to have included some remains of a defunct Roman canal bed.[97]) In Cordoba, farmers were already drawing from canals and natural *wadi*s to make Cordoba into a highly productive and much-admired agricultural landscape, at which point the caliph intervened to create a system that could serve his new palace (and others) as well as deliver more water to the growing city of Cordoba and its congregational mosque.

How to Level a Canal

To build a successful canal requires practical geometrical knowledge applied at a large scale. As the water conduit traverses the terrain, it must adapt to the topographical irregularities and soil conditions, progressively descending until it reaches its destination. Moreover, it must flow at a steady and very gradual gradient (about 1:100 or less, depending on water volume and the quality of the canal bed). If the canal does not have an adequate gradient, the water cannot move, but if the gradient is too steep, turbulence ensues, causing the canal bed to erode and the water to overflow. Because irrigation by canal depended entirely on the ability to construct the canal with a proper slope, many of the agricultural manuals provide instructions on levelling: for example, the Iraqi author Abu Bakr Aḥmad ibn Waḥshiyya (d. 870), and the Andalusi authors Ibn Bassal (mid-eleventh to early twelfth centuries), Ibn al-Awwam (late twelfth century), and Ibn Luyun (d. 1349).[98]

In mountainous environments such as Yemen, the Maghreb, or the Iberian Peninsula, canals are typically cut into the side of a mountain, running as though along a contour line. Sometimes a tunnel will be excavated to direct the canal through a hill, but less costly and thus preferable is an open-air waterway. Where the canal has to pass over an existing ravine or a *wadi*, an aqueduct may be built or, more rarely, a siphon. Where the water runs too rapidly downhill or falls in a cascade, it may be calmed by a flow-regulating basin (Figure 33). These strategies for conducting water over distances were employed in the ordinary rural landscape as well as in urban and palatine contexts. For example, to allow

---

[97] L. J. García Pulido, *El Territorio de la Alhambra* (Granada: Patronato de la Alhambra y Generalife, 2013).

[98] Ibn Waḥshiyya, *Kitāb al-filāḥa an-Nabaṭiya*, ed. T. Fahd, 3rd edition (Damascus: Institut Français de Damas, 1998); partial translation by J. Hämeen-Anttila, *The Last Pagans of Iraq. Ibn Waḥshiyya and his Nabatean Agriculture* (Leiden: Brill, 2006); Ibn Bassal, *Libro de Agricultura*, ed. and trans. J. M. Millás Vallicrosa and M. Aziman (Tetuan: Instituto Muley al-Hasan, 1955), chapter 4; Ibn al-Awwam, *Libro de Agricultura*, ed. J. I. Cubiero Salmerón of the 1802 translation by J.A. Banqueri (S.L.: Empresa Pública para el Desarrollo Agrario y Pesquero de Andalucía, 1999), chapter 3, article 1; Ibn Luyun, *Tratado de Agricultura*, no. 15.

Islamicate Environments

Figure 33 In the Alpujarra, as the surface canal rushing down from the mountain drops in level, a regulating basin slows its speed (photo: H. Varden)

the Acequia Real ("royal canal") to cross the ravine that separates the late thirteenth-century Generalife Palace from the Alhambra in Granada, a one-arched aqueduct springs overhead (Figure 34). Also at the Generalife, regulating basins were used to control the water in the handrails of the Water Stairway (Figure 35). At each landing, the exuberant downward rush is checked when the water drops into a small basin and achieves a more level gradient as it encircles the landing before continuing its downward flow.

The calculation of the correct rate of incline was accomplished using relatively simple levelling tools, the most common of which was the suspended triangle, as explained and illustrated by Ibn Luyun. Using this technique, a pole was stuck in the ground and a second pole stuck in the ground ten yards away from the first. A rope

Figure 34 A one-arched aqueduct carried the canal that passes over the ravine separating the Generalife (on the left) from the Alhambra (on the right) (photo: D.F. Ruggles)

was stretched between them with a large triangle, called a *murjīqal*, suspended from it, apex pointing downward (Figure 36). A vertical groove etched in the triangle clearly marked its center line. Hanging from the spot where the vertical groove met the triangle's upper edge was a plumbline. By tilting the rope so that the plumbline aligned with the triangle's groove, a true horizontal could be achieved. At that point, a sighting was made along the now horizontal level toward a point farther in the distance. A gradient could then be calculated for optimal flow.[99]

---

[99] Ibn Luyun, *Tratado de* Agricultura, no. 15. However, S. C. Stiros cautions that in systems that measured slope across as many as 80 kilometers of uneven terrain, there were bound to be errors. The most likely of these was the refraction error, which occurred due to variations in temperature, humidity, or air pressure as light passes through air layers. The best way to correct for refraction errors was to take repeated and redundant observations from a variety of positions ("Accurate measurements with primitive instruments: The 'paradox' in the qanat design," *Journal of Archaeological Science* 33 [2006]: 1058–64).

Figure 35 In the water stairway at the Generalife the water drops into the small depression on the lower left, slowing its flow (photo: D.F. Ruggles)

Another leveling device described by Ibn Luyun exploited the naturally level surface of a body of water. He wrote: "In a flattened place, fill a basin with uniform edges with water. A long stick is spread over the basin; you look at it, placing your eyes on the stick, and you place a mark at the place where your gaze falls."[100] Like the triangular *murjiqal*, once the stick was aligned with the perfect horizontal provided by the water surface, the eye could look across it toward a more distant point which could then be marked.

If levelling techniques were essential in the design of canals of any distance, they were also useful in creating flat plots of land. In his agricultural treatise, Ibn Bassal described the *murjiqal* not with respect to canal construction but as a tool for levelling farmland so that water would flow evenly to every corner of the field. He also gave the rather obvious advice that in levelling one must take earth from the higher levels and carry it to the lower levels. Finally, he described a tool called a *jaruf* (harrow) which was a board that was suspended and dragged between two oxen to smooth the soil's surface.[101]

---

[100] Ibn Luyun, *Tratado de* Agricultura, no. 17.   [101] Ibn Bassal, *Libro de Agricultura*, p. 61.

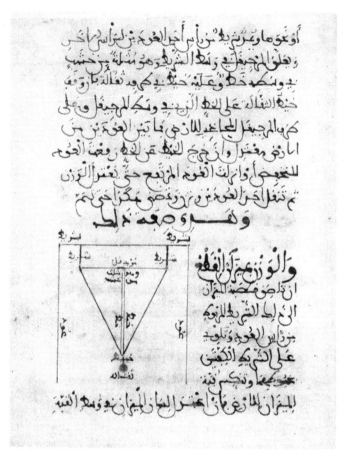

Figure 36 Ibn Luyun's diagram of a *murjiqal*, or levelling device (courtesy of the Escuela de Estudios Arabes, CSIC)

4 Technology: The *Qanat*

A third way of obtaining water came from the *qanat*, a system that combined vertical wells with subterranean and surface conduits. A *qanat* is a tunnel that runs underground to carry water from the source point to a destination that may be many kilometers distant. Because the destination may be far out in the desert, and because the *qanat*'s subterranean course offers little visible trace of its existence other than the air vents that dot the surface of the land, the *qanat* can cause water to appear from the sand like a mirage (Figure 37). The *qanat* seems to have its origins in Iran at least as early as the Achaemenid Empire (sixth to fourth centuries BCE), possibly earlier, and its initial application seems to have been to drain away water seepage during mining operations. The technology then spread to Syria,

Islamicate Environments

Figure 37 In Yazd, a *qanat* emerges to the surface after running underground for miles (photo: D.F. Ruggles)

the Arabian Peninsula, and India; the Romans carried it across northern Africa; and Muslims brought the technique to the Iberian Peninsula and Sicily.

At first glance, a *qanat* may seem to emerge from underground and thus constitute another case of "water from below." But since aquifers have higher levels at the foot of mountains where the *qanat* originates, and much lower levels out in the landscape where the *qanat* ends, the water canal is actually higher at its point of origin than at its mouth. Technically, it flows downhill.

The construction of a *qanat* begins at the foot of a hill or mountain with one or more mother wells that is excavated to tap into the aquifer which, due to the snow melt and runoff from the mountain, is fairly high at that point (Figure 38). Donald Hill gives a detailed explanation of how the rest of the *qanat* is built,

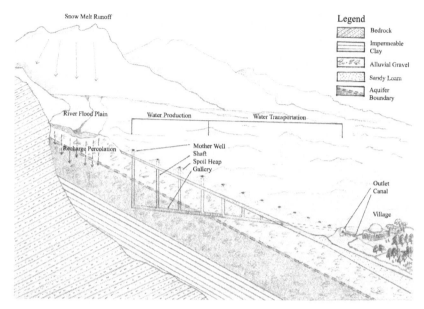

Figure 38 *Qanat* diagram (drawing: B. Schleicher)

summarized as follows.[102] The engineer, known as a *muqannīs*, drops a rope down the shaft of this initial well to determine the distance between ground level and the water's surface. Then, about 30 meters away, a second well is excavated, this one serving as the first of what will be a long line of ventilation shafts. A survey is made to establish the horizontal level and the decline from the mother well to the ventilation shaft, and the rope is marked accordingly. This is repeated over and over until the engineer reaches the end of the rope, at which point – if his calculations have been accurate – the ground surface is the same as the level of the water in the mother well. Hill explains that the actual discharge point at the mouth of *qanat* must be below this spot and yet above the agricultural fields where the water is to be used. The underground tunnel must run at a very slight slope that declines less than the water table itself and less than the surface of the land above ground. Modern observations of *qanats* suggest that for a short *qanat*, the gradient should be between 1:500 and 1:1500, whereas for a long one crossing flat terrain the gradient will be between 1:6000 and 1:8000.[103]

At this point, after having excavated a sequence of wells, the workers begin to dig the horizontal tunnel, working backward from the mouth to the mother well to avoid until the ultimate moment the dangerous torrent of water that the

---

[102] Hill, *A History of Engineering*, 33–35.   [103] Stiros, "Accurate Measurements," 1059.

mother well will release. Meanwhile, as the tunnel is being excavated, any water that does begin to seep into it is conveniently evacuated by running along the slope to the discharge point. Once the *qanat* is completed, Hill assessed the average rate of flow to be about 45–90 liters per second. For comparison, modern field observation in Oman calculated that a typical *qanat* can yield 20–50 liters per second, and a particularly sizable system could have an output of quite a bit more.[104] Because the *qanat*'s rate of flow can be very energetic, Hill notes that it may be constructed in a zigzag path to slow it down.[105]

The initial investment in construction is extraordinarily high, demanding a significant financial investment and a skilled work force that is subjected to considerable danger, but once constructed, no human or animal labor is required to move the water because it flows gravitationally for twenty-four hours a day. It transports copious amounts of water, often providing irrigation to an entire settlement that, in an otherwise dry environment, flourishes like a natural oasis. Moreover, in hot climates, the *qanat* has the advantage over open surface canals in that the water does not evaporate. But like the system of surface canals, the *qanat*'s water had to be distributed fairly. To monitor the amount of water that a stakeholder received from the larger water system, a reliable system of measurement was essential. One system apportioned water based on volume, in which each share was measured in terms of proportion to the whole, while the other apportioned it based on time, in which the share was determined by a set period of water flow. Whether the allocation was made by time or by volumetric proportion, the systems did not simply mirror but actually constituted the network of relations among stakeholders.

Allocating Irrigation Water with Clocks

In a system that relied on a temporal schedule, the main canal flowed constantly but was controlled by means of temporary barriers that could be closed or opened as needed. In this way, the canal waters could be directed to a specific stakeholder for a stipulated period of time called a *dawla* ("turn"). In the Alpujarra region of al-Andalus, the *habices* (a post-conquest record of endowments that stemmed from the Muslim *waqf*) of the Iglesia de Mecina offer a detailed look at how farms were assessed and provided with water in one community. One of the farms was described in

---
[104] E. J. Dybro, "Islamic Law and the Development of Agricultural Settlement in Oman. On the Question of Tradition and Development," in *Workshop in Political Theory and Policy Analysis* (Bloomington: Indiana University, 1995), 6; Hill, *A History of Engineering*, 35–36.
[105] Hill, *A History of Engineering*, 35–36.

the document as consisting of 3.5 *marjales* of flat land (equivalent to 1,837.5 square meters), for which the farmer received one quarter of the canal's water on Fridays.[106] Similarly, in the Syrian region of Hama, the water that was lifted by noria was distributed on an eight-day cycle, each recipient getting water for a period of time ranging from three to thirty-six hours, depending on the size of the plot.[107]

When there was enough water in a good season, each of the stakeholders in such a network got water in turn, usually starting with those who were closest to the main canal or water source. In Yemen's terraced landscape, where the water flowed along a *wadi* and was allocated in timed units, the term used to describe the sequence of turns was: *al-aʿlā fa-l-aʿlā* or "the one who is highest, then the one who is next highest."[108] This had the immediate effect of creating a hierarchy according to one's position upstream or downstream of all the other stakeholders along the *wadi*. There were palpable outcomes to this because in periods of drought the *wadi* could run dry, leaving those at the end of the line with nothing. To create a bit more of a balance, the calendar was adjusted to give those downstream a bit more time, but even so, in such a system the position of one's land vis-à-vis the *wadi* affected its value. Often, the farmers in the lower areas sold their plots to farmers upstream, because the later could either divert some of their water to the lower holding or could divide their crops with those plants needing the most water cultivated at the top of the *wadi* and those needing the least at its base.[109]

The amount of elapsed time was measured by simple instruments, such as the sundial, in use since time immemorial. Requiring no complex calculations or mathematical expertise, a sundial is nothing more than the visual measure of the shadow cast by a vertical element contraposed on a fixed surface. In the area of Ghayl Ba Wazir in Yemen, Hehmeyer observed that

---

[106] L. L. Padilla Mellado, *Libro del Apeamiento de los Habices del Alpujarra, de las Tahas de Ferreyra, Poqueyra y Jubiles* (Granada: Ayuntamiento de la Alpujarra de la Sierra, 2012), 78; citing *Libro del Apeamiento de los Habices del Alpujarra, de las Tahas de Ferreyra, Poqueyra y Jubiles que los apeó Benito de Carrión, escribano. Año 1527. Los Bienes Habices de Mecina del Buen Varón, Godeo y Yegen*.

[107] Zaqzouq, "Les Norias," II: 355.

[108] N. Salameh, "Customary Water Rights in Medieval Wadi Zabid: Some Legal Cases on *al-ʿadil biʾl-qanaʿah*," *Proceedings of the Seminar for Arabian Studies: Papers from the Thirty-Second Meeting of the Seminar for Arabian Studies held in London, July 16–18, 1998*, 29 (1999): 137–42.

[109] Hehmeyer, *A History of Water Engineering*, 84–87; R. B. Serjeant, "Some Irrigation Systems in Hadramawt," *Bulletin of the School of Oriental and African Studies* 27.1 (1964): 36. On modern changes to the system of allocation in response to desertification, see F. van Steenbergen, and A. al-Weshali, "A New World, More Equity: Changing Water Allocation in Wadi Zabid, Yemen," *The Water Channel*, https://thewaterchannel.tv/thewaterblog/a-new-world-more-equity-changing-water-allocation-in-wadi-zabid-yemen/ (accessed 1 May 2024).

the vertical could be the body of the farmer himself, an example of what David King had called "folk astronomy."[110] In her observation, if the farmer was told that his turn of the water flow on a given day would be 25 percent of the daylight period, say from approximately 9:00 a.m. to noon, then the *qanat* supervisor would arrive at the appointed time and measure the farmer's shadow as the farmer stood with his left side toward the sun. The shadow would be about seven feet in length, and the water outlet would be opened to allow the water to enter the farmer's fields. When the shadow decreased to two feet in length – which was the equivalent of about three hours – the water flow would be cut off.[111] This same procedure seems to have been used in Granada where the irrigation turn of one canal in 1492 lasted from sunrise "until a man's shadow attains a length of eight feet ... which will be more or less two hours after sunrise."[112] In contemporary Sanaba (Yemen), the turn lasted for about three hours and was repeated every seventeen days.[113]

In the Islamic world, the more sophisticated sundial is typically associated with mosques where there was a clear need to determine the times for the five daily prayers as well as the beginning and end of the Ramadhan fasts. In al-Andalus a fragment (about half) of one of the oldest sundials was found in Cordoba near the Roman tomb on the city's western wall (Figure 39).[114] Made of white marble, it bears the name of its maker, Ahmad ibn al-Saffar, an astronomer working in Cordoba, thus suggesting a date c. 1000 CE.[115] The fact that it recorded not only the twelve hours of the day but also the times for midday and afternoon prayer, and that it was made of an expensive material, confirms that this sundial was not intended for the dusty agricultural fields but was used in the mosque. However, its reliance on the sun's position was the same as that used for agriculture.

In the field, a sundial was a crude measure of time, although, as seen in the example previously, sometimes a crude measure was good enough. In the Islamic agricultural context, the daylight hours were divided into 12 units, but

---

[110] I. Hehmeyer, 'Diurnal Time Measurement for Water Allocation in Southern Yemen," *Proceedings of the Seminar for Arabian Studies* (*Papers from the Thirty-Eighth Meeting*) 35 (2005): 87–96; D. A. King, "Science in the Service of Religion: The Case of Islam," *Impact of Science on Society* 159 (1990): 246.

[111] Hehmeyer, "Diurnal Time Measurement," 89–90; a similar process is described by Varisco, 'Irrigation in an Arabian Valley,' 29.

[112] T. Glick, "Medieval Irrigation Clocks," *Technology and Culture* 10.3 (1969): 424–8, citing M. Garrido Atienza, *Los alquezares de Santafe* (Granada: Universidad de Granada, 1893), 65.

[113] Varisco, "Irrigation in an Arabian Valley," 29.

[114] D. Cabanales, "Relojes de sol hispano-musulmanes," *Al-Andalus* 23 (1958): 391–406.

[115] D. A. King, "Three Sundials from Islamic Andalusia," *Journal for the History of Arabic Science* 2.2 (1978): 358–92.

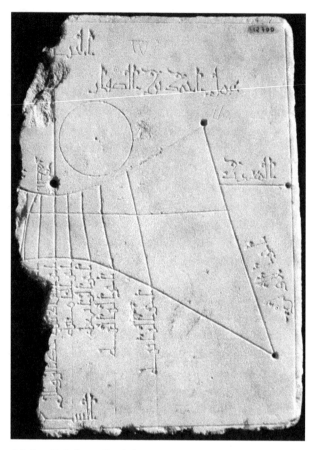

Figure 39 Sundial from Cordoba (courtesy of the Museo Arqueológico de Córdoba)

since the length of day varies seasonally and by location, these units were not fixed lengths of time but proportional measurements. Therefore, in winter the daylight "hours" were shorter than during the summer.[116] Time, in this context was not an absolute measure; what mattered was the allotted time relative to one stakeholder vis-à-vis that of the next. However, *qanats* and canals flow all day and night, and the sundial cannot keep track of who uses the water at night. In those environments, the water might be collected overnight in cisterns, or a system of apportionment might be preferred that relied on proportion or some combination of proportional and temporal measurement.[117] All of

---

[116] D. A. King, "Los cuadrantes solares andalusíes," *El Legado Científico Andalusí* (Madrid: Museo Arqueológico Nacional, 1992), 89–102; Hehmeyer, "Diurnal Time Measurement."

[117] A. M. Carballeira Debasa, "Agrarian Measures in the Kingdom of Granada before and after the Castilian Conquest: The Lands of the Alpujarra," *Rural History* 33.1 (2022): 61–73.

these strategies were employed in Granada where the water for the Albaicín quarter came from the canal called the Acequia de Aynadamar. The canal flowed through an agricultural region where the farms along its path got their turns. But 25 percent of the total volume was designated for the village of Viznar from April to October, between the hours of noon and sundown, thus reflecting both volumetric and temporal systems of distribution. At night, all the water went to the city, filling its network of cisterns.[118]

In addition to sundials, there were mechanical clocks such as the automata (discussed in Section 2) made for elite audiences with the leisure to enjoy their clever complexity. However, the clocks used for irrigated agriculture were mechanically very simple, typically using small quantities of controlled water flow to measure larger ones. One type of water clock (or clepsydra) was the *tarjahar*, a sinking bowl or inflow system, in use as early as 1500 BCE in Babylonia.[119] This type of clock converted time into material volume so that it could be visually observed. The device consisted of a bowl with a hole in its bottom that floated in a larger basin or container of water until enough water filled the bowl to sink it, constituting one unit of time (Figure 40). Subunits of time could be marked on the side of the bowl, a determination that had to be made on the basis of repeated observation rather than a more abstract measurement since the rate of discharge decreases as water level drops.

A second type was the *qadus* (plural: *aqdās*). This device consisted of a noria bucket with a hole in its bottom that was filled with water and suspended until it emptied, each bucketful representing a temporal unit. It was a variant of the sinking bowl in that it used the visibility of volume (one bowlful or one bucketful) to represent time in tangible terms. Al-Bakrı described how irrigation was regulated with the *qadus* at the oasis of Touzer (Tunisia) in the eleventh century:

> The procedure is that he who has the irrigation turn (*dawla al-saqī*) repairs to a *qadus* in the bottom of which is a hole as large as the teasing-bow [a device for carding cotton] which clogs it, and it is filled with water and suspended [and the clog removed]. He irrigates his plot and his garden from the canals until the water in the *qadus* runs out. They fill it up again, and they know that a full day's irrigation amounts to 192 *aqdās*.[120]

---

[118] Trillo San José, "A Social Analysis of Irrigation in Al-Andalus," 163–83.
[119] al-Hasan and Hill, *Islamic Technology*, 55–57.
[120] Glick, 'Medieval Irrigation Clocks,' 426–7, citing al-Bakri, *Dikr bilad Ifriqiya w'al-Magrib* ed. M. de Slane (2nd rev. ed.; Algiers: Adolphe Jourdan, 1913), 48–49.

Figure 40 Water clock from Yazd (Iran) (photo: D.F. Ruggles)

The *qadus* system must have required constant vigilance since the bucket, which had to be refilled 192 times according to al-Bakri, emptied every 7.5 minutes.

Finally, in his study of irrigation clocks, Thomas Glick lists the sand clock, or hourglass – not adopted until the fourteenth century – and the mechanical clocks that were in use in southern Spain by the late fifteenth century. Perhaps the "irrigation bell" heard in Granada in the 1490s relied on a mechanical timekeeping device. In the mid-nineteenth century the bell was still in use and described by an observer:[121]

> On the top of the highest tower of the Alhambra, commanding a glorious view over the fertile plain below stretching away to the west, and of the Sierra Nevada, soaring up in majestic forms to the south-east, is suspended a large bell, which is struck every five minutes from sunset to sunrise. There is a conventional system by which the peasant, counting the number of beats, knows exactly the hour, and when it is time to open or close his watercourse. The bell is said to be heard through the still night over all the *vega*, or irrigated plain.

---

[121] C. C. Scott-Moncrieff, *Irrigation in Southern Europe* (London: E. & F.N. Spon, 1868), 118.

He noted that although the bell was given to Granada by Queen Isabel after the conquest of the city in 1492, it restored "a Moorish institution of far older date." This is plausible, given the care with which the Christian conquerors sought to understand and maintain water systems of the Muslims.

Irrigation based on "turns" demanded a careful accounting of time. Although the sundials that were made for mosques represented a scientific approach to time keeping and were made using careful measurements so that the lines inscribed on any sundial were uniquely correct for that place, the "measured man" type of sun dial, the sinking bowl and the *qadus* represent a different attitude toward time that was more suitable for the peasant farmer. For the latter, what mattered was not the precise time of the day or the specific day of the year but an articulation in immediately graspable terms of when and for how long the farmer would get water.

Allocating Irrigation Water by Volume

Another system relied on proportional quantities of water. In the Ghouta quarter of Damascus, the regions of Valencia and Murcia in eastern Spain, and the Timimoun region of Algeria, each stakeholder got a fixed percent of the total volume of water. The percentages owned by any one person might be more or less than those owned by another person for reasons having to do with land ownership and family mergers, but in other respects it was based on equality. When the canals ran full, everyone got enough to water their fields, and when the canals slowed to a trickle, everyone suffered.

The general intent was fair distribution. In the Fayyum, the distribution calculation acknowledged that downstream recipients were likely to get less water than those upstream due to conveyance loss caused by evaporation of the canal water under the hot sun and water seepage. In compensation, the downstream recipients were allowed to have wider apertures in openings of the canals that led to their lands. Overall, according to the study by Rapoport and Sahar, "the system of rights was intended to ensure that each of the villages along the gravity-fed canals received a fair share of water and that downstream communities were not disadvantaged."[122]

The proportional method of distribution required a mechanism that could turn one large flow into two or more smaller ones (and subdivided the smaller flows as well) that could be directed to different areas (Figure 41). This device, known as a *kasria* in the Maghreb, *partidor* in post-conquest Spain, and

---

[122] Rapoport and Sahar, "Irrigation in the Medieval Islamic Fayyum," 21.

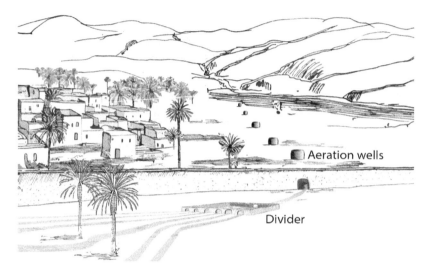

Figure 41 A *qanat* brings water to the surface, where it is divided by a *kasria* (drawing: M. Mallula).

maqsam in Egypt, played an enormously important role in the water system both with respect to technology and social organization. Unlike dams which might be made of mud so they could be erected or removed as needed, the *kasria* was more likely to be made of stone or mortar so that it would remain stable and visible to all of its users from one year to the next. In the Fayyum, the dividing might be accomplished through the use of a perforated board (*khashaba*). According to an eleventh-century account of how the recipients divided such water: "The board is divided by gaps according to their water rights. In each gap water enters according to what is due its owner, whether a fifth or a tenth."[123] Whether stone or wooden board, the *kasria* not only performed the act of dividing the water; it also stood as the material reification of those divisions, each aperture transforming the abstract concept of a given percent into a tangible reality. As the canal flowed into the *kasria*, it entered into one end of a rectangular or triangular tank that allowed the settlement of the silt that the water carried. This tank required regular cleaning. At the other end it passed through a comb with several apertures that split the flow into much smaller canals. At this point, the water changed from the status of being a commonly

---

[123] Rapoport and Sahar, "Irrigation in the Medieval Islamic Fayyum," 21, citing al-Mawardi, *Kitab al-Ahkam al-sultaniyya wa-l-wilayat al-diniyya*, ed. Samr Mustafa Rabab (Beirut: al-Maktaba al-'Asriyya, 2000), 202–3. The board was also employed in the Alpujarra, Carballeira Debasa, "Agrarian measures in the Kingdom of Granada before and after the Castilian Conquest," 61–73. See also Caponera, *Water Laws*, 23.

Figure 42 Water divider in the Timimoun oasis (photo: Godong / BSIP/ Alamy)

held good in the main canal, to something that "belonged" by right to each of properties served by the smaller canals.

An actively used water divider in the Timimoun oasis (Algeria) shows this shift: the water introduced into the community is held collectively in a rectangular basin before being split into equal shares of water flow (Figure 42).[124] However, the physical alterations made to the *kasria* and its small canals show that, while the system was set up with seventeen shares initially, some form of negotiation occurred over the years as several owners acquired multiple shares. Consequently, although there are still seventeen units, there are now only ten recipients.

Water dividers were necessary for systems that distributed on the basis of proportion; but they could also be useful in any hydraulic network in which a main canal had to be split into secondary canals, regardless of whether those canals ultimately delivered water on a temporal or proportional basis. Figure 43 shows the bed of a water channel in the mountainous Alpujarra region of Spain. When the main canal enters on the lower right, it is split into two streams by a large, permanent, stone wedge. In the

---

[124] B. Remini, J. Albergel, and B. Achour, "The Garden Foggara of Timimoun (Algeria): The Decline of Hydraulic Heritage," *Asian Journal of Water, Environment and Pollution* 12.3 (2015): 51–57.

Figure 43 A canal (*acequia*) is split into two streams (photo: D.F. Ruggles)

present day, each of these flows can be temporarily blocked by dropping a metal plate (as seen in the upper canal), thus diverting the water into the other canal. In the medieval period, the barrage would be effected simply by a large clump of mud, a slab of stone or a fabric-wrapped board, and indeed the procedure is so simple that it is still in use (Figure 44).

The System of Justice

Just as farmers with irrigated lands needed reliable ways of measuring the flow of the irrigation canal into their plots, they also needed procedures for resolving the disputes that inevitably occurred. Sometimes, this meant appealing to a higher authority. The aforementioned Yemeni tax register reveals that the Rasulid sultans contributed to the irrigation infrastructure of the *wadi* area, paying for the reconstruction of dams when they were destroyed by particularly forceful water flows. Some sort of recognized authority with a broad perspective was needed to ensure that farmers upstream got their water while also protecting those downstream from flooding. In this way, the sultan aided stakeholders who, while united by

Islamicate Environments 71

Figure 44 In the Agdal gardens outside of Marrakesh, the flow of an irrigation canal can be blocked and redirected by a simple stone barrier
(photo: D.F. Ruggles)

their shared dependency on the *wadi*, may have had only minimal direct social relations.[125]

Given the level of dependency on the water, it is not surprising that lawsuits were brought when water rights were not respected. Analyzing a 1520 Yemeni work on water disputes, Nadim Salameh has examined cases in which water rights were abridged: in some cases, dams were built too solidly so that they could not be dismantled to send water to the next field, and in others the complaint pertained to neighbors who flooded their land too generously, leaving an insufficient amount for the next in line. The most common type of conflict occurred between farmers with adjacent plots in which one took precedence in

---

[125] Hehmeyer, *History of Water Engineering*, citing M. Jazim, *Irtifaʿ al-dawla al-Muʾayyadiyya*.

the sequence of irrigation flow.[126] In another Yemeni treatise on water rights that compiled and contrasted the opinions of two authorities, problems regarding changes in the environmental conditions of the irrigation system were addressed. One case stemmed from a farmer's petition to raise the outlet for the channel that flowed out of his land because the rise in silt levels in his terraced plot meant that less inundation occurred. Perhaps because they were applying customary versus written law, the legal respondents did not concur in their answers. One said that the farmer could exercise his right to the water by raising the water outlet's level as needed, but the other said that if the land level rose due to the build-up of sediment, it was the farmer's own responsibility to clear the land of the problematic silt. The farmer was not allowed to tinker with the canal's water outlet.[127]

In al-Andalus, traces of social conflict can be seen in the *kitab al-filaha*. Although the authors of the manuals did not claim expertise in law, they knew that arguments over water rights would inevitably arise in any irrigation society. Ibn Bassal saved his advice regarding conflict for the last chapter of his treatise, writing, "If someone digs a well in one place, and it produces sufficient water, and then another person opens another well next to the first, such that the [subterranean] vein of water from the first well is insufficient for the second … this can be the cause conflict among the irrigators." He then proceeds to outline a very complicated technique for assessing the precise impact of the second well on the first, explaining all the many variables that must be taken into consideration in order to resolve the dispute.[128] Here too, the resolution was a matter of customary practice, not canonized in law. The goal was not to punish bad actors but to get the system back in balance.

In the period immediately following the Christian conquest of al-Andalus, there are two ways that the social residue of irrigation can be seen to have endured despite the change in political regimes. One is the *ordenanzas* of sixteenth-century Granada, and the other is the Tribunal de Agua in Valencia.

When Granada fell to Christian rule in 1492, the shift from one political regime to the other was felt acutely in urban areas and in those lands that had been actively wrested through military conquest. But in much of the Alpujarra, which was rugged and remote and thus resistant to conquest, life continued as

---

[126] Hehmeyer, *History of Water Engineering*, 92–93; Salameh, "Customary Water Rights in Mediaeval Wadi Zabid," 137–42.

[127] N. Salameh, "Water Rights in 16th Century Hadramawt – One Question, Two Answers. The Legal Opinions of Ibn Hajar al-Haytami and al-Bakri al-Siddiqi," *Proceedings of the Seminar for Arabian Studies (Papers from the Thirty-Fourth Meeting of the Seminar for Arabian Studies held in London, July 20–22, 2000)* 31 (2001): 215–20.

[128] Ibn Bassal, *Libro de Agricultura*, 227–8.

before with irrigation canals flowing, taxes assessed, and crops harvested. We know this because the agrarian practices of the farmers in the Alpujarra were carefully observed and recorded by the new Spanish government so that order and prosperity could be maintained. Thus, although the documentation comes from a later period, it reflects older Andalusi practices that had continued uninterrupted from before the conquest.

In order to understand the Andalusi system of land and water management, which relied on laterally connected tribal associations and differed substantially from the more hierarchical Christian feudal system, the new governors drafted *ordenanzas*, regulatory codes that recorded how things should be run, "because that's how it was done in the times of the Moors."[129] The *ordenanzas* took the form of a compilation of norms regarding the cleaning and regulation of the water canals. Initially drawn up in 1501, they were modified in 1535 and 1538 and onward, a sign that the information that they contained remained important enough to merit updating. Moreover, because people argued about the interpretation of the rules set forth in the *ordenanzas*, a council called the Juzgado Privilegiado de las Aguas was formed in 1501 to adjudicate disputes over water. The council comprised five men: the mayor and four irrigators.[130]

Similarly in Valencia, a water tribunal has met weekly since at least 960 (Figure 45).[131] The magistrates of the Tribunal de Agua meet in public outside the portal of the cathedral, where the city's congregational mosque once stood. Each magistrate is responsible for one of the main canals in Valencia (and in one case for two canals), and to qualify to serve as magistrate, he must work his own land. In other words, this is a court run by the farmers themselves. At the weekly gathering (which has become a very popular celebration of citizen democracy), the *aguacil*, or officer, stands and calls out, *Denunciats de la Séquia de Quart?* ("Denunciations regarding the Quart Canal?"). If no complaints are fielded for the Quart canal, he proceeds to the next, and so on. One curious aspect of this is that

---

[129] *Ordenanzas que los muy Ilustres, muy magníficos Señores de Granada mandaron guardar, para la buena gobernación de su república* (Impressas en Granada, en la Imprenta Real de Francisco de Ochoa, 1672), folio 215v, cited in A. Orihuela Uzal and C. Vílchez Vílchez, *Aljibes Públicos de la Granada Islámica* (Granada: Ayuntamiento de Granada, 1991), 30. On the *ordenanzas* and water law, see C. Trillo San José, "Entre Rey y la Comunidad: El Agua del Albaizín (Granada) en la Edad Media," *Meridies: Revista de Historia Medieval* 10 (2012): 151–74.

[130] M. T. de Diego Velasco, "Las Ordenanzas de las Aguas de Granada," *En la España Medieval* 4 (1984): 249–76.

[131] V. Giner Boira, *El tribunal de las Aguas de la Vega de Valencia* (Valencia: Tribunal de Aguas, 1960). There is not much evidence for the actual date of the tribunal, and as Glick explains, the function of the tribunal may have changed over time. But he asserts that it "was a customary, informal institution of long evolution" (*Irrigation and Society*, 64–68).

Figure 45 In the Tribunal de Aguas, which meets weekly outside the south portal of the Cathedral of Valencia, each canal is represented by its own magistrate (photo: D.F. Ruggles)

if a complaint is levied against one of the canal magistrates, as has happened in the past, the magistrate must step outside the tribunal's circle to answer the charge and cannot resume his post until the grievance has been resolved. Impartiality is guaranteed by having the magistrates of the canals on the left bank of the river pass judgment on cases pertinent to the right bank, and vice versa.

The statutes that they uphold have been passed down orally for centuries and were written down in the eighteenth century. They pertain to matters such as water theft, damage to the canal's architecture, women using the irrigation canals for doing laundry, failing to maintain the canal free of debris, and other such infractions. The actual court proceeding is entirely oral because its goal is not to exact a current or future punishment but to ensure a smoothly working system in the present day. Indeed, Thomas Glick, who made a thorough study of Valencia's water tribunal, states that the function of the tribunal "was not judgment, but consultation among those who best knew the custom of the huerta" (farmland), and that the tribunal "was an embodiment of the basic precept of consensual authority in irrigation."[132]

---

[132] Glick, *Irrigation and Society*, 68.

5 Irrigation Societies and Agricultural Expertise

The Yemeni, Egyptian, Andalusi and other cases described here underscore the many ways that water shapes society, especially when that society is almost wholly dependent on irrigation for its livelihood. We have seen that the need for irrigation creates related requirements such as cooperative agreements regarding water distribution, judicial systems to handle disputes, skill in leveling and *qanat* design to plan the routes of watercourses, and mechanisms for keeping track of time. All of this demanded some degree of proficiency, consisting of a combination of knowledge with the ability to manage social and ecological variables. The concept of skill conjures up an expert whose ability to plan on a large scale distinguishes him or her from the ordinary farmer, a peasant whose only imaginable contribution to the irrigated landscape was labor. This begs the question that has permeated the field of irrigation studies for the past fifty years: Were irrigation societies formed through top-down planning, in which expertise, capital, the judiciary, and the markets were all controlled by a central authority, the peasants merely supplying corvee labor to build the physical structures of dams and canals? Or were such societies built from the ground up, designed by the people who, living on the land that they farmed, had nuanced knowledge about what plants to grow in which environments and understood how to coax the most water out of their environment?

From a materialist perspective, there can be no doubt that water has an agency that affects the social and even political environment. The unidirectional flow of a river, *wadi*, or canal casts the stakeholders along its course in relationships in which each one is either upstream or downstream from the next. In such a structure, the stakeholders are positioned according to their place in the spatial and temporal flow of the water, with social consequences: if a farm or residence upstream takes more than its stipulated share (as in so many of the cases brought before the water tribunals) or polluted the water in some way (as in the case of women washing laundry in Valencia's irrigation canals), the people downstream will feel the impact and raise their voices in protest. The force felt in such cases is neither entirely top-down nor bottom-up, but a force exerted by the environment itself. The sun's heat, the scarcity of rain, geology, soil, contours of the land, and native vegetation demand adaptation from the people living in that place. This attribution of agency to the environment complicates the questions posed here. Instead of a binary choice between a centralized state imposing an irrigation system on a people, or a community of farmers negotiating among themselves to create one, the identification of the environment as a central player takes at least part of the question of agency out of the political realm and places it in the material world. This is a new perspective, enabled by the development of environmental materialism as a field. Until recently, the debate regarding agency in irrigation societies was stuck in a largely sociopolitical framework.

The Power of the State

Karl Wittfogel's *Oriental Despotism* (1957) was a foundational inquiry into the relationship between large-scale irrigation systems and human societies.[133] In it he described a model of centralized state authority, based on the need to control water for irrigation in arid lands, finding these "hydraulic societies" in ancient Egypt, ancient Mesopotamia, imperial China, Peru under the Incas, and Islamic lands under the Mughals and the Abbasids, among others. Paradoxically, although the book's thesis stemmed from Marxist and Hegelian analysis in which Wittfogel had been steeped in his earlier years in Germany, it gained wide readership in the United States and eventually Europe for its critique of postwar Communist totalitarianism in the Soviet Union and China, examples of failed Marxist revolutions.[134]

Wittfogel's theory was that the construction of canals, *qanats*, and major dams in premodern history had to have been top-down creations, built as one piece, the work of a strong centralized government, which the author saw primarily in Eastern societies. In this model of the "hydraulic society," the state controls the most important natural resource and consequently the economy, the military, and all forms of expertise, all of which depended on that resource. Wittfogel's analysis did not explain the *historical* reasons for why such a state might emerge in such a region but simply maintained that a despotic and comprehensive form of the government would inevitably emerge in agricultural societies reliant on irrigation to farm the land and that it would follow a path of imperial expansion. The model was one of environmental determinism. As summarized by Eva Hunt and Robert Hunt in one of the many scholarly rebuttals to *Oriental Despotism*:

> The basic need to control water, administer the construction and maintenance of massive water works (by corvee labor), allocate capital expenditures and

---

[133] K. Wittfogel, *Oriental Despotism: A Comparative Study of Total Power* (New Haven: Yale University Press, 1957). An excellent summary of Wittfogel's arguments can be read in E. Hunt and R. Hunt, "Irrigation, Conflict, and Politics: A Mexican Case," in T. E. Downing and M. Gibson (eds.), *Irrigation's Impact on Society* (Tucson: The University of Arizona Press, 1974), 129.

[134] T. Glick, "Historia del regadío y las técnicas hidráulicas en la España Medieval y moderna. Bibliografía comentada. I," *Chronica Nova* 18 (1990): 191–221. A good summary of Wittfogel's political formation is given in J. L. Wescoat, "Wittfogel East and West: Changing Perspectives on Water Development in South Asia and the United States, 1670–2000," in A. Murphy and D. Johnson (eds.), *Cultural Encounters with the Environment* (Lanham: Rowman and Littlefield, 2000), 110–13.

resources over water, as well as to schedule the distribution to keep the system going efficiently, gives those persons in the irrigated society who occupy crucial role synapses in the irrigation system, expansive powers in other domains of social life.[135]

For Wittfogel, the state flourishes because the peasants themselves are incapable of organization or collaboration.

If the "hydraulic society" theory was persuasive in some quarters, it was because Wittfogel could point to states where the stranglehold on natural resources did indeed lead to political repression. The example for which Wittfogel had the most familiarity was imperial China where he observed that "every commoner family was expected on demand to provide labor for hydraulic and other public services."[136] And there were other societies where centralized state control was evident. Examining Abbasid-era Iraq through the lens of an eleventh-century anonymous treatise (and writing before the publication of *Oriental Despotism*), Claude Cahen described a "highly organized State enterprise, with an army of bureaucrats, engineers and surveyors, controlling a very large labour force, whose productivity and rates of pay were closely specified."[137]

Regarded from the perspective of the state's interest in and control of key resources, the Bahr Yusuf canal that brought the Nile water to the Fayyum in Egypt in the thirteenth century was so essential for the prosperity of the Fayyum (and the feeding of Egypt) that we would expect that the Ayyubid state would have used it to impose control over the crops grown at the oasis. But, as we have seen, the official who visited the region in the mid-thirteenth century saw no such government oversight. Instead, he observed a communally maintained irrigation system in which labor and funds were locally and voluntarily obtained under the direction of a few village men who simply met as needed. Rapaport and Sahar conclude that "the allocation of water rights in mediaeval Fayyum was remarkably egalitarian," attributing this to a strong clan-based social fabric rather than the control of a centralized government.[138]

Local Administration

Perhaps because the theory of "hydraulic societies" was so overarching in its proposal of a political system that could be applied around the world, it was rejected by scholars who pointed to specific cases where the opposite

---
[135] Hunt and Hunt, "Irrigation, Conflict, and Politics: A Mexican Case,"129.
[136] Wittfogel, *Oriental Despotism*, 25.
[137] C. Cahen, "Le service de l'Irrigation en Iraq au début du XIeme siècle," *Bulletin d'études orientales* 13 (1949–51): 117–43. The Abbasid state was one of those identified by Wittfogel as being a hydraulic society.
[138] Rapoport and Shahar, "Irrigation in the Medieval Islamic Fayoum," 29.

phenomenon occurred: communities that *self*-organized in response to water scarcity, driving modest improvements and leading to shared investments in land development. In the Alpujarra, for example, Carmen Trillo's studies have shown that farming did not occur in the form of huge latifundia controlled by powerful lords but as smaller land holdings managed by individual farmers that coexisted with some larger holdings owned by the sultan and his family.[139] Because the most productive and most highly valued land was irrigated, and because such hydraulic systems extended far beyond the boundaries of any farmer's individual plot, farmers had to develop methods for collaborating in their installation. In the Timimoun oasis, the social organization of ordinary landowners was made manifest in the divider that split the water flow into 17 streams or shares. Varisco's observations of farming communities in the Yemeni highlands showed that water resources were in the hands of the farmers themselves who needed no direct supervision, so that "[p]ower is spread rather than concentrated."[140] In sum, Wittfogel's sweeping thesis of irrigation leading to tyrannical states clearly was not the only, or even the primary, template for governance in arid landscapes.

However, Wittfogel was right in one important respect: dependence on irrigation is a powerful incentive for organization. We have seen that societies develop norms, social relationships, laws, new technologies, even clocks as they organize both urban and rural space around the presence or absence of water. But he was wrong in his insistence that such organization was necessarily driven from the top down by a powerful elite. He completely ignored the power of the peasant.

History records many examples of peasant knowledge, as when in the eleventh century, a farmer presented the taifa ruler of Seville with four particularly large melons. The ruler "was very much surprised to see so fine a fruit, and began to question the peasant, who answered that those melons did not always grow to so great a size, but that such dimensions could easily be obtained by cutting off all but ten of the branches of the plants, and then supporting the remaining stems by means of props of wood."[141] The farmer was describing the simple technique of disbudding (still practiced today), in which all but a few of the budding fruits are removed in order to direct the plant's energy into the remaining ones. The exchange revealed the peasant's skill as a gardener, and the king's ignorance, a hierarchy of expertise that is the reverse of what Wittfogel had predicted.

Farmers also made key decisions and applied their knowledge when they encountered new types of agriculturally useful plants that moved across the

---

[139] C. Trillo, "El tiempo del agua. El regadío y su organización en la Granada islámica," *Acta historica et archaeologica mediaevalia* 23–24 (2002–2003): 237–86.
[140] Varisco, "Irrigation in an Arabian Valley," 34.   [141] Al-Maqqari, *History*, I:62–3

Figure 46 Two types of asparagus, in al-Ghafiqi, *Kitab fi'l-adwiya al-mufrada* (McGill University/Bridgeman)

Islamic Mediterranean, as documented in the *kitab al-filaha* and botanical treatises (Figure 46). The farmer could now choose between planting eggplant or spinach, or between varieties of asparagus, carefully observing the specific requirements of the plant and the environmental conditions that were available for cultivating it. Indeed, the plants listed in Ibn Bassal's eleventh-century treatise on agriculture include 177 species that ranged from basic foods such as barley and sorghum, to spices such as cumin and caraway, and even included ornamental flowers (although many of these, such as the crocus and rose, also were used for flavoring and perfumery).[142] Most of the plants were not cash crops intended for

---

[142] Ibn Bassal, *Tratado de agricultura*, trans. J. M. Millas Vallicrosa and M. Aziman (Tetuan: Instituto Muley el-Hasan, 1955); for a discussion of the plant lists, see J. Esteban Hernández Bermejo, and

export to distant consumers through coastal ports, but food crops for local consumption. The introduction and dissemination of new plants beyond the basic triad of wheat, olive, and grapes not only gave ordinary people a more varied diet and presumably better health, it also gave farmers greater autonomy with respect to what to plant. Moreover, since each crop was planted and harvested in a different month, the variety undermined the government's ability to calculate yields in advance and collect agricultural taxes in anticipation of those yields.[143]

Glick entered the discussion about the social impact of irrigation technology with his book *Irrigation and Society in Medieval Valencia* in 1970.[144] In that study of the irrigation systems of Valencia from the thirteenth century to 1500, he mined the archive of documentary evidence that had survived from the period of Christian rule (beginning with Aragon's conquest of Valencia in 1238) in order to trace continuity between that period and the earlier period of Islamic rule. But he was quick to point out that the continuity and stability of the institutional framework did not mean paralysis.[145] There was an active and ongoing effort to distribute water fairly and to settle the disputes that inevitably arose. In Valencia's Tribunal del Agua, the procedure was entirely oral and so effective (according to boasts) that conflicts never had to proceed to an actual court of law answerable to the state. We recall that those who settled the disputes, that is, the Tribunal's magistrates, were themselves stakeholders in the irrigation system. Yet it was because some members of some irrigation communities did eventually take recourse in the court of law to insist upon their rights and negotiate with their neighbors, that the written record of their demands and thus their social organization was preserved and could be studied by Glick. Whether adjudicated by citizen-magistrates or the court of law, it was those closest to the land who could understand the stakes of the conflicts and the best way to resolve them. Glick wrote: "[I]n the huerta of Valencia, social control has traditionally rested in the collective will and institutions of the irrigators themselves."[146]

The "Design" of Irrigated Landscapes

Among the many scholars refuting Wittfogel's sweeping thesis, Miquel Barceló also took up the question of the peasant and the environment, armed with years

---

E. García Sánchez, "Economic Botany and Ethnobotany in Al-Andalus (Iberian Peninsula: Tenth-Fifteenth Centuries), an Unknown Heritage of Mankind," *Economic Botany*, 52 (1998): 15–26.

[143] Watson, *Agricultural Innovation*; C. Trillo San Jose, "A Social Analysis of Irrigation in Al-Andalus: Nazari Granada (13th–15th centuries)," *Journal of Medieval History* 31 (2005): 163–83.

[144] Glick, *Irrigation and Society in Medieval Valencia*; Spanish translation: *Regadío y sociedad en la Valencia medieval* (Valencia, Del Cenia al Segura, 1988).

[145] Glick, *Irrigation and Society*, 3.   [146] Glick, *Irrigation and Society*, 5.

of experience as an archaeologist. Of his numerous publications on irrigation in medieval Valencia and Murcia, one had the character of a manifesto: "El diseño de espacios irrigados en al-Andalus: un enunciado de principios generales" in 1989 (appearing ten years later in English as "The Design of Irrigation Systems in al-Andalus: A Statement of General Principles").[147] In it Barceló wrote that irrigation is both a technology and a social practice and that, while it can either be developed by the farmers themselves or imposed by the state, the fact of the environment's aridity is not in and of itself a sufficient explanation for the kind of irrigation system that the community adopts or the kind of society that ensues. Moreover, he categorically rejected the tendency among archaeologists to try to determine the origins of such systems – as, for example, attributing both the hydraulic technologies and the irrigation systems in al-Andalus to Roman origins – pointing out that those quests always begin with the uninterrogated premise that planning and technology must be the work of a well-developed state. The belief that effective systems necessarily come from top-down state planning is a convenient perspective for modern European (and North American) nations who historically gained power through colonial domination. As a counter argument, he pointed to research in northern Africa that found that many techniques for managing water in arid environments were indigenous practices, "a common response to a common set of problems and restrictions."[148] In addition to political prejudices, he noted technological ones, posing the question of whether the enthusiastic adoption of aerial photography by archaeologists in the mid-twentieth century could have contributed to the erroneous assumption that canal networks were continuous systems of large-scale irrigation infrastructure because from such a distance they seemed to be so.[149]

Having presented irrigation systems as local productions, he then asserted that "they are the result of an initial design requiring not only a correct understanding of the environment, but also adequacy to the agricultural aims of the peasant group constructing the system."[150] He explained "design" in terms of the basic and immutable principle that guides water: its gravitational flow from

---

[147] M. Barceló, "El diseño de espacios irrigados en al-Andalus: un enunciado de principios generales," in *El Agua en zona áridas: arqueología e historia, Vol. 1, Actas del I. Coloquio, Almería,14–15–16 diciembre 1989* (Almería: Instituto de Estudios Almerienses de la Diputación de Almería, 1989), xv-l. This was later translated and published as "The Design of Irrigation Systems in al-Andalus: A Statement of General Principles," in M. Barceló, H. Kirchner, R. Martí, and J. M. Torres, *The Design of Irrigation Systems in al-Andalus* (Barcelona: Departament d'Historia et les Societats Precapitalistes i d'Antropologia Social, Universitat Autònoma de Barcelona, 1998), 9–22.

[148] Barceló, "El diseño," vvii. In this respect, he particularly admired the work of B. D. Shaw on northern African irrigation communities: "Water and Society in the ancient maghrib: Technology, Property and Development," *Antiquités Africaines* 20 (1984): 121–73.

[149] Barceló, xviii.   [150] Barceló, xviii.

Figure 47 Canal in the Alpujarra (photo: H. Varden)

source or catchment site which determines the placement and gradient of the irrigation canals. From its point of origin to its destination, the slope and volume of the water flow must be calculated and known in advance, making it nearly impossible to add on to such a system in most instances (Figure 47). An irrigation system has a potential configuration and a maximum reach due to elevation and gravity that is recognized at the moment of its construction. Beyond that, its capacity for expansion is limited by the amount of water produced by the source and the elevation and topography that allows the canals to run downhill. Because the initial source is limited with respect to its output, and because the land will eventually flatten out, the system cannot be expanded simply because its dependents wish to put more land into irrigated cultivation. Every canal has a natural end. Thus, the installation of such a system must reflect careful planning and forethought. This is precisely what happened on a smaller scale in Granada when the first Nasrid ruler founded the Alhambra on the Sabika Hill in the mid-thirteenth century. Although the eleventh-century Acequia de Axares already existed, drawing water from the Darro River at a point upstream, this canal, and a second one that later drew from it, served the lower areas of the Albaicín. The Axares canal system could not serve the Alhambra, because of the palace's higher elevation, and thus, a new canal, the Acequia Real, drawing from a point more than six kilometers upstream, was built sometime shortly before 1238. It is this later canal, with two that later split off from it, that fills the palace's many pools and animates its fountains.[151]

The term "design" raised alarms in some quarters because it sounded as though Barceló was identifying a system like Wittfogel's: necessarily at a large scale, created by one central authoritative designer, and insensitive to environmental differences. But as Barceló himself explained in a rebuttal to one such critique, by "design" he meant simply that a hydraulic system is installed with a comprehensive structure in mind. Expansion may be possible to a limited extent, but the system cannot be installed as a fraction of an unrealized whole because of the topographic requirements for the system – as the Alhambra example demonstrates. These are environmental factors from which the design cannot be separated.[152]

A key point in his argument is that irrigation requires a "social decision."[153] It has to include the peasants themselves, who are perfectly capable of making informed choices. He noted that farmers are very good at selecting the right plants for the dry or irrigated environmental niche where they are to be cultivated. Thus, he wrote, the mere fact of an environment's aridity, no matter how extreme, cannot in and of itself explain the system of irrigation built and practiced there because it overlooks the decisions made by the farmers.

6 Conclusion: An Environmental Perspective on the Islamicate Mediterranean

This study of the Islamicate Mediterranean environment stands at the intersection of history, geography, archaeology, anthropology, and political theory. But even more important than the diverse disciplinary perspectives is the emphasis on the intersection of material and social culture. In my inquiry into the physical structure of canals revealed by archaeologists, and the studies of wheel and *shaduf* technologies provided by engineers, these things have been treated not as isolated objects and practices, but as factors that shape society and help human beings adapt to the environment.

In writing about the environment, it is important to pay attention to the sources of information because such sources – especially textual documents – reflect the world view of their authors. Historical texts are written by literate writers for literate readers who are usually urban and invariably educated, and as such they reflect the social milieu of their authors who, if they farmed, did so

---

[151] García Pulido, *El Territorio de la Alhambra*.
[152] M. Barceló, "Acerca de Nada. Consideraciones sobre dos artículos de S. Gutiérrez," in *Agricultura y Regadío en el-Andalus: Síntesis y Problemas. Actas del Coloquio, Almería, 9 y 10 Junio 1995* (Almería: Instituto de Estudios Almerienses de la Diputación de Almería, 1995), 273–91.
[153] Barceló, "El diseño," xv; trans. "The Design," 9.

with an awareness of the world beyond the boundaries of their residences. Yet the fact that authors such as Abu'l Khayr and Ibn Luyun engaged in actual practice is important because it shows that farming and gardening were not disdained by the elite. Quite the contrary. Nonetheless, when modern historians pay attention to farmers at all, they tend to characterize them as laboring bodies lacking agency, perhaps because so few modern historians have themselves ever wielded a trowel or watched a seedling grow. History itself is often divided into periods defined by ruling dynasties – both in contemporary chronicles and in modern histories of the Islamic world – and in those, farmers are important only insofar as they produce the taxes with which great monuments such as Madinat al-Zahra' and the Qala Bani Hammad were built. As sites where plants and agricultural technologies from the larger landscape were employed, and where vestiges of the buildings, water systems, and landforms still exist, such palaces could reveal a lot about the environmental practices of the tenth and eleventh centuries, but instead they are more likely to be discussed in terms of architectural typology and patronage. For this reason, the *kitab al-filaha* genre and texts such as the thirteenth-century Yemeni tax register, with its diagram of the *wadi* canals, merit our attention.

The disciplinary approach of archaeology is more grounded than that of history. As a form of investigation that requires mucking about in the dirt, it is necessarily a bottom-up method for studying agricultural society. But archaeology, too, has its blind spots, sometimes treating buildings as works of architecture without paying sufficient attention to the larger environmental context that enabled the settlement. Without water, Qasr al-Hayr's olive orchards, and thus its economy, could not have existed. More than a tension between architecture-as-object and landscape-as-context, there is a tension here between object and *system*. In his studies of irrigation in arid environments, Barceló had insisted on the importance of hydraulic archaeology in which agricultural spaces were seen as interconnected systems rather than as a collection of individual waterwheels, canals, terraces, and *qanats*. He and his colleagues Helena Kirchner and Carmen Navarro integrated the two perspectives of "qanat as material object" and "qanat as social organization."[154] As Barcelo explained: "irrigation is not only a technical fact, but also the result of a social decision."[155] Glick phrased it slightly differently, characterizing technique as a mechanical way of doing something, but technology as a "cognitive system."[156]

---

[154] H. Kirchner and C. Navarro, "Objectivos, métodos y práctica de la arqueología hidráulica," *Archeología Medievale* 20 (1993), 122, citing Barceló's work in the 1980s on water systems in Mallorca.
[155] Barceló, "El diseño," xv; "The Design," 9.
[156] T. Glick, "Hydraulic Technology in al-Andalus," in S. K. Jayyusi (ed.), *The Legacy of Muslim Spain* (Leiden: Brill, 1992), 983.

In my past works on Islamic gardens and landscapes, I have explained the importance of treating landscapes as systems in which the social perspective of the observer (whether as author, reader, or viewer) affects the thing observed, and in which the framing of the landscape through a window, a map, or text calls the landscape into being as a discrete object.[157] I have also underscored the importance of the scale of analysis, noting how attention to scale can enhance our understanding of the way that sites such as the Alhambra or the Taj Mahal received water and what the presence of water meant. Depending on how narrowly we focus our attention, we will either perceive the building as an architectural envelope that contains fountains and gardens, or we will look beyond the enclosure walls to the nearby river and canals, tracing them from destination to source. Our gaze may even take in the mountains and the clouds that hover over the mountains, dropping the rain and snow that fills the canals that feed the fountains and gardens in the city below (Figure 48).[158] The emphasis on scale is a geographical strategy. While it encourages the conceptualization of a boundless space, it recognizes the natural and bounded systems within that space and thus does not conflict with Barceló's definition of an irrigation system with defined limits. Whereas the scalar magnitude to which I am referring is that of climate, rainfall, and rivers, Barceló was referring to an environmentally specific hydraulic system made by humans. The difference is between natural and constructed systems.

Environmental Agency

Attention to scale enables us to see agency operating at various levels, from the farmer to the state and the environment itself. Having examined the limitations of Wittfogel, who attributed all form of agency to the state, and having considered some of the studies that rejected his globalizing model of "hydraulic societies," we can now move away from the choice between a top-down model of state agency and a bottom-up model of peasant agency to consider a third form of agency: that of the environment itself. This seems to be where Barceló was heading with his description of design, a model that recognized the inherent natural limits of any given environment where an artificial irrigation system is constructed. He grounded his argument on the ineluctable fact of gravity: "The fundamental structure of a system is the result of a design which, necessarily based on gravity as its founding element, articulates the point of water's catchment, the direction and slope of the supply canals, the location of the regulation reservoirs, and the sites of any mills."[159]

---

[157] Ruggles, *Gardens, Landscape, and Vision*, 208.
[158] D.F. Ruggles, "From Garden to Landscape: Lessons from the Taj and the Alhambra," *International Journal of Islamic Architecture* 10.1 (2021): 89–98; Ruggles, "The Aljibe del Rey."
[159] Barcelo, "El diseño," xxv; "The Design," 14.

Figure 48 The snow-capped Sierra Nevada mountains from which the Alhambra Palace receives its water (photo: D.F. Ruggles)

There is a reciprocal relationship between the environment and humankind in which the environment exerts force in the form of gravity, precipitation, and sunlight which mold the very existence of humans. In turn, humans likewise exert force on the environment as they seek to guide the path of water, level the earth's surfaces, and domesticate exotic plant species. But instead of characterizing this interplay of forces in terms of simple cause and effect, we might consider the more interactive model of "agency" provided by Bruno Latour and Jane Bennett (among others), scholars in the field of New Materialism.

In defining things, New Materialism does not differentiate between organic and inorganic, living and inert, or subject and object. In place of these, New Materialism gives us the agent, actant, or actor, all of which have some sort of force, whether active or latent. For Latour, "an actor is what is *made* to act by many others," which – using the image of the theater as his example – includes the script, the stage, the lighting, and the audience.[160] In other words, the actor is not an absolute identity but one that is temporarily produced by virtue of performing in a play. Likewise, the play exists as a performance because there

---

[160] B. Latour, *Reassembling the Social: An Introduction to Actor-Network-Theory* (Oxford University Press, 2005), 45–46. In this deconstruction of the actor, he echoes M. Foucault, "What Is an Author?" *The Foucault Reader* (originally written 1969; New York, 1984), 101–20.

are actors to speak the lines of the script on stage. Each is contingent on the other. With this definition, Latour shifts the focus from the thing as object (a grammatical position) to the unstable thing that comes into being through association with other things, in other words, a variable in a social context. Thus, things elude the status of subject or object, which, in any case, are positions that can be reversed: if the dog bites me, I can respond by kicking the dog, the agency of the dog or me changing according to the position in the grammatical structure. Instead, the animal and human beings become "interveners."[161] As interveners, their power is not located in the individual animal or human body or closed social group but instead occurs across a diverse field in which they act upon each other.[162]

Similarly, Bennett explains that because there is no stability – no fixed sequence of cause and effect – any given field is constantly being made through the input and force of each of its members.[163] Using the electrical grid as her example, she describes it as a field that is "vibrant," pulsing with the input of each constituent part, resulting in "distributive agency." With respect to the human-world relationship where our own subjectivity is at stake, she describes things as having agency in their ability to hail us, to attract our interest.[164] As used in both of these examples, "agency" is that which has power, force, or impact, but it does not necessarily imply consciousness or subjectivity. What it does is to allow us to consider things outside of the fixed grammatical and ontological structure of subject-verb-object, in which the subject has force which it exerts on the object.

In some respects, the claims of New Materialism are not new; observers of animism and fetishism know quite well the kind of agency that mere things can exert.[165] And simply by looking at an ice cube melting in the sun, or a plant responding to sunlight, it is obvious that the properties of things are affected by their interactions with the rest of the world (Figure 49). In the words of Tim Ingold, "Bringing things to life, then, is a matter not of adding to them a sprinkling of agency but of restoring them to the generative fluxes of the world of materials in which they came into being and continue to subsist."[166] By this he hopes to avoid the split between human history and

---

[161] J. Bennett, *Vibrant Matter: A Political Ecology of Things* (Durham: Duke University Press, 2010), 9, citing B. Latour, *Politics of Nature*, 75.

[162] To this process of "re-association and reassembling" Latour gave the name "Actor Network Theory" (ANT), *Reassembling the Social*, 1–17; see also Bennett, *Vibrant Matter*, 21–23.

[163] Bennett, *Vibrant Matter*, 21–23.

[164] J. Bennett, "Powers of the Hoard: Further Notes on Material Agency," in J. Cohen (ed.), *Animal, Vegetable, Mineral: Ethics and Objects* (Washington, DC: Oliphaunt Books, 2012), 237–69.

[165] T. Ingold, "Materials against Materiality," *Archaeological Dialogues* 14.1 (2007), 11–12.

[166] Ingold, "Materials against Materiality," 12.

Figure 49 In the spring, sunlight and warmth signal to the orange tree that it is time to bear flowers and, eventually, fruit (photo: D.F. Ruggles)

natural history and instead to see humans and non-humans in an "interplay" of "mutual involvement."[167] For the environmental historian, these various perspectives on New Materialism help dissolve the traditional split between humans and nonhumans, a category which includes everything from animals to soil, water, plants, and clouds. It demands that we pay attention to the ways that the environment imposes itself on us as an actor, and not simply as an object that is acted upon.[168]

We have seen that in the early centuries of Islam the intelligent management of water extended the growing season and converted the desert into fertile agricultural land where orchards could be grown (Figure 50). The introduction of new varieties of plants from the East gave farmers greater flexibility and choice in the plants that they grew and certainly must have made for a more resilient agricultural economy, especially in al-Andalus which gained fame for

---

[167] T. Ingold, "Anthropology Comes to Life," in T. Ingold (ed.), *Being Alive: Essays on Movement, Knowledge and Description* (London: Routledge, 2011), 9.

[168] To assign agency to the environment at a time when human actions have wrought such damage on the climate and natural environment may seem disingenuous. But given that the current crisis is the result of brash human behavior that saw the environment as simply a collection of resources to be consumed, it may be fruitful to change the perspective from one of absolute human control over the environment to one of a human-nature partnership.

Islamicate Environments

Figure 50 In the desert of Algeria, farmers use the dunes as wind barriers, stabilizing them with palm fronds and irrigating the trees with well water (photo: George Steinmetz)

its productive landscapes and handsome gardens. All over the early Islamic world, as the agricultural economy prospered, poets praised the beauty of their verdant surroundings and waterwheels and fountains became much more than merely utilitarian machines. But it is important to recognize that the new plants were not simply plunked into an optimal place in the preexisting landscape. When the plants were introduced, the land had to be made more accommodating, with more or less irrigation, terraced or flattened fields, and new types of fertilizer. In other words, the landscape was not a stable context into which new botanical objects were introduced: both the land and the plants were changing in response to each other because both were actors in a vibrant field. Moreover, the farmers themselves were changed in the process. They built up a corpus of knowledge for the cultivation, propagation, and storage of the new plants. They created laws for land ownership and developed social systems for the distribution of water and adjudication of conflicts. They too were shaped by vibrant environmental forces that acted upon them.

Instead of making distinctions to differentiate among inanimate things, the natural world, and human society, this volume has kept its focus on humans *in* the environment. While people impact the landscape, they are also driven into social relations by that same environment by virtue of spatial proximity, upstream/downstream water flows, shared investments, and their desire for justice as achieved through litigation and appeal to local councils. In an irrigation society, farmers push against natural conditions to wrest maximum yield from the land with machinery and tools, while the state pushes the farmers to pay taxes on those yields and to supply urban markets. But these technical and social pressures occur within a larger environment system. Just as Latour described the actor not as a lone player but an element in an "actor-network," so too, we can think of the peasant as being part of a network that included the farmer together with the land, canals, trees, seed storage, *kasria*s, knowledge webs, markets, and tax assessors. These constitute the agricultural landscape of the early Islamicate world.

To understand the technical system of irrigation in an environment where water is a precious resource, we must look both to the environmental conditions and the human social system. Likewise, to understand human society in such a context, we must understand both the irrigation technology and the environment. Far more than mere context or material resource, the environment is a key force in the formation of the material and the social world.

Bibliography

Abu'l-Khayr. *Kitāb al-Filāḥa ou Le Livre de la Culture: Notice et extraits traduits par A. Cherbonneau, éclaircissements par H. Pérès* (Bibliographie Arabe-Française 5), A. Cherbonneau and H. Pérès (eds.) (Alger: Carbonel, 1946).

Anderson, Perry. *Lineages of the Absolutist State* (London: Verso, 1979).

Arnold, Felix, Alberto Canto García, and Antonio Vallejo Triano. *Munyat ar-Rummaniya: ein islamischer Landsitz bei Córdoba. Teil 1. Palastanlagen* (Wiesbaden, 2015). Spanish translation *La almunia de Al-Rummāniyya (Córdoba)* (Seville: Consejería de Cultura, Junta de Andalucía, 2021).

Ashtor, E. "Levantine Weights and Standard Parcels: A Contribution to the Metrology of the Later Middle Ages," *Bulletin of the School of Oriental and African Studies* 45.3 (1982): 471–488.

Barceló, Miquel. "El diseño de espacios irrigados en al-Andalus: un enunciado de principios generales," in Lorenzo Cara Barrionuevo (ed.), *El Agua en zona áridas: arqueología e historia, Vol. 1, Actas del I. Coloquio, Almería, 14–15–16 diciembre 1989* (Almería: Instituto de Estudios Almerienses de la Diputación de Almería, 1989), xv–l.

Bennett, Jane. "Powers of the hoard: Further notes on material agency," in Jeffrey Cohen (ed.), *Animal, Vegetable, Mineral: Ethics and Objects* (Washington, DC: Oliphaunt Books, 2012), 237–269.

Bennett, Jane. *Vibrant Matter: A Political Ecology of Things* (Durham: Duke University Press, 2010).

Bolens, Lucie. *Les méthodes culturales au moyen âge d'après les traités d'agronomie andalous: Traditions et techniques* (Geneva: Médecine et Hygiène, 1974).

Bolens, Lucie. "Agriculture in the Islamic World," in Helaine Selin (ed.), *Encyclopedia of the History of Science, Technology and Medicine in Non-Western Cultures* (New York: Springer, 1997), 20–22.

Borsch, Stuart J. "Nile Floods and the Irrigation System in Fifteenth-Century Egypt," *Mamluk Studies Review* 4 (2000): 131–145.

Bourgeon, Oriane, Clémence Pagnoux, Stéphane Mauné et al. "Olive Tree Varieties Cultivated for the Great Baetican Oil Trade between the 1st and the 4th Centuries AD: Morphometric Analysis of Olive Stones from Las Delicias (Ecija, Province of Seville, Spain)," *Vegetation History and Archaeobotany* 27.3 (2018): 463–476.

Bukhari n.d., *Al-Adab al-Mufrad*, no. 304, no. 891, and no. 1182.

Butzer, Karl. "The Islamic Traditions of Agroecology: Crosscultural Experience, Ideas and Innovation," *Ecumene: Journal of Environment, Culture Meaning* 1 (1994): 7–50.

Cabanelas, Dario. "Relojes de sol hispano-musulmanes," *Al-Andalus* 23 (1958): 391–406.

Cahen, Claude. "Le service de l'irrigation en Iraq au début du XIe siècle." *Bulletin d'études orientales* 13 (1949–51):117–143.

Caponera, Dante. *Water Laws in Moslem Countries* (Rome: Food and Agriculture Organization of the United Nations, 1954).

Carballeira Debasa, Ana Maria. "Agrarian Measures in the Kingdom of Granada before and after the Castilian Conquest: The Lands of the Alpujarra," *Rural History* 33.1 (2022): 61–73.

Chambrade, Marie-Laure, Mohamed Al-Dbiyat, and Bernard Geyer. "Water Infrastructures: Ancient Water Infrastructure," in Ronald Jaubert, M. Saadé, M. Al Dbiyat, and A. H. Asaad (eds.), *Atlas of Orontes River Basin*, 2nd ed. (Geneva: Graduate Institute, 2022): pp. 35–43.

Colin, Golin S. "La noria marocaine et les machines hydrauliques dans le monde árabe," *Hespéris* 4 (1932): 22–60.

Coomaraswamy, Ananda K. *The Treatise of al-Jazari* (Boston: Museum of Fine Arts, 1924).

Córdoba de la Llave, Ricardo. "La noria de la Albolafia, el Alcázar y el Guadalquivir: un paisaje urbano de la Córdoba medieval," *Al-Mulk* 18 (2020): 415–428.

Creswell, K. A. C. *Muslim Architecture of Egypt*, 2 vols. (Oxford: Oxford University Press, 1940).

Despois, J. J. "Bir, iii, the Maghreb," in *The Encyclopaedia of Islam*, 2nd ed., 12 vols. Vol. I (1960): 1231–1232.

Diego Velasco, María Teresa de. "Las Ordenanzas de las Aguas de Granada," *En la España Medieval* 4 (1984): 249–276.

D'Ottone, Arianna. "Il manoscritto Vaticano arabo 368, Hadit Bayad wa Riyad. Il codice, il testo, le immagini," *Rivista di Storia della Miniatura* 14 (2010): 55–70.

Douglas, T. D., S. J. Kirby, R. W. Critchley, and G. J. Park. "Agricultural Terrace Abandonment in the Alpujarra, Andalucia, Spain," *Land Degradation & Rehabilitation* 5 (1994): 281–291.

Dybro, Jens E. "Islamic Law and the Development of Agricultural Settlement in Oman. On the Question of Tradition and Development," in *Workshop in Political Theory and Policy Analysis* (Bloomington: Indiana University, 1995): 1–21.

El-Samarraie, Husum Qawam. *Agriculture in Iraq during the 3rd Century, A.H.* (Beirut: Librairie du Liban, 1972).

The Filaha Texts Project. www.filaha.org.

Foucault, Michel. "What Is an Author?" in Paul Rabinow (ed.), *The Foucault Reader* (originally written 1969; New York: Pantheon, 1984), 101–120.

Fuks, Daniel, Oriya Amichay, and Ehud Weiss. "Innovation or Preservation? Abbasid Aubergines, Archaeobotany, and the Islamic Green Revolution," *Archaeological & Anthropological Sciences* 12.2 (2020): 1–16.

García Gómez, Emilio. "Sobre agricultura arábigo andaluza," *Al-Andalus* 10 (1945): 127–146.

García Pulido, Luis José. *El Territorio de la Alhambra* (Granada: Patronato de la Alhambra y Generalife, 2013).

García Pulido, Luis José. "The Mastery in Hydraulic Techniques for Water Supply at the Alhambra," *Journal of Islamic Studies* 27.3 (2016): 355–382.

García Sánchez, Expiración. "Cultivos y espacios agrícolas irrigados en al-Andalus," in Lorenzo Cara Barrionuevo and Antonio Malpica Cuello (eds.), *Agricultura y Regadío en el-Andalus: Síntesis y Problemas. Actas del Coloquio, Almería, 9 y 10 Junio 1995* (Almería: Instituto de Estudios Almerienses de la Diputación de Almería, 1995), 17–37.

Gayangos. *See* al-Maqqari.

Giner Boira, Vicente. *El tribunal de las Aguas de la Vega de Valencia* (Valencia: Tribunal de Aguas, 1960).

Glick, Thomas. "Dos documentos medievales referents al Tribunal de las Aguas," *Boletin de la sociedad Castellonense de Cultura* 43 (1967): 81–84.

Glick. Thomas. "Historia del regadio y las técnicas hidráulicas en la España Medieval y moderna. Bibliografía comentada. I," *Chronica Nova* 18 (1990): 191–221.

Glick, Thomas. "Hydraulic Technology in al-Andalus," in Salma K. Jayyusi (ed.), *The Legacy of Muslim Spain* (Leiden: E. J. Brill, 1992), 974–986.

Glick, Thomas. *Irrigation and Society in Medieval Valencia* (Cambridge, MA: Harvard University Press, 1970).

Glick, Thomas. "Levels and Leveling: Surveying Irrigation Canals in Medieval Valencia," *Technology and Culture* 9.2 (1968): 165–180.

Glick, Thomas. "Medieval Irrigation Clocks," *Technology and Culture* 10.3 (1969): 424–428.

Grabar, Oleg, Renata Holod, James Knustad, and William Trousdale. *City in the Desert: Qasr al-Hayr East* (Cambridge, MA: Harvard University Press, 1978).

Hamilton, Richard W. *Khirbat al-Mafjar: An Arabian Mansion in the Jordan Valley* (Oxford: Clarendon Press, 1959).

al-Hasan, Ahmad Y. (ed.). *Kitab al-Hiyal: The Book of Ingenious Devices* (Aleppo: University of Aleppo, 1981).

al-Hasan, Ahmad Y., and Donald R. Hill. *Islamic Technology: An Illustrated History* (Cambridge: Cambridge University Press, 1986).

Hegel, Georg Wilhelm Frederich. *Lectures on the Philosophy of World History*, 2 vols. (Originally 1822; Oxford: Oxford University Press, 2011).

Hehmeyer, Ingrid. "Diurnal Time Measurement for Water Allocation in Southern Yemen," *Proceedings of the Seminar for Arabian Studies* (Papers from the Thirty-Eighth Meeting) 35 (2005): 87–96.

Hehmeyer, Ingrid. *A History of Water Engineering and Management in Yemen* (Leiden: Brill, 2019).

Hehmeyer, Ingrid. "Physical Evidence of Engineered Water Systems in Medieval Zabid," *Proceedings of the Seminar for Arabian Studies* (Papers from at the Twenty-Eighth Meeting of the Seminar for Arabian Studies held at Oxford, July 21–23, 1994, 25 (1995): 45–54.

Hernández Bermejo, J. Esteban and Expiración García Sánchez. "Economic Botany and Ethnobotany in Al-Andalus (Iberian Peninsula: Tenth-Fifteenth Centuries), an Unknown Heritage of Mankind," *Economic Botany* 52 (1998):15–26.

Hernández Giménez, Félix. "Restauración en el molino de la Albolafia de Córdoba," *Al-Mulk* 2 (1961–1962): 161–173.

Hill, Donald. *A History of Engineering in Classical and Medieval Times* (London: Croom Hill, 1984).

Hill Donald (trans. and ed.). *Ibn al-Razzaz al-Jaziri, the Book of Ingenious Mechanical Devices* (Boston: D. Reidel, 1974).

Hunt, Eva, and Robert Hunt. "Irrigation, Conflict, and Politics: A Mexican Case," in Theodore Downing and MacGuire Gibson (eds.), *Irrigation's Impact on Society* (Tucson: The University of Arizona Press, 1974), 129–157.

Ibn al-Awwam. *Libro de Agricultura*, ed. José I. Cubiero Salmerón from the 1802 translation by. José A. Banqueri (S. L.: Empresa Pública para el Desarrollo Agrario y Pesquero de Andalucía, 1999).

Ibn Bassal. *Tratado de agricultura*, trans. José M. Millás Vallicrosa and Mohamed Aziman (Tetuan: Instituto Muley el-Hassan, 1955).

Ibn Battuta. *The Travels of Ibn Battuta, A.D. 1325–1354*, ed. H. A. R. Gibb. 3 vols. (originally 1958; New York: Routledge, 2016).

Ibn Ghalib. "La descripción de Córdoba de Ibn Galib," trans. Joaquín Vallvé Bermejo, in *Homenaje a Pedro Sáinz Rodríguez*, vol. 3 (Madrid: Fundación Universitaria Española, 1986), 669–679.

Ibn Idhari. *Bayan al-Mughrib fi ikhtisar akhbar muluk al-Andalus wal-Maghrib*, trans. Ambrosio Huici Miranda, 2 vols. (Tetuan: Editorial Maroquí, 1954).
Ibn Khalduun. *The Muqaddimah: An Introduction to History*, trans. Franz Rosenthal (Princeton: Princeton University Press, 1967).
Ibn Luyun. *Ibn Luyūn: Tratado de agricultura*, trans. Joaquina Eguaras Ibáñez (Almería: Editorial Universidad de Almería, 2014).
Ibn Luyun. *Kitāb ibdā' al-malāḥa wa-inhā' al-riyāḥa fī uṣūl ṣinā'at al-filāḥa* (Escuela de Estudios Árabes, Ms. 14). http://aleph.csic.es/imagenes/mad01/0006_PMSC/html/001349506.html#page/1/mode/2up.
Ingold, Tim. "Anthropology Comes to Life," in Ingold (ed.), *Being Alive: Essays on Movement, Knowledge and Description* (New York: Routledge, 2011), 3–14.
Ingold, Tim. "Materials against Materiality," *Archaeological Dialogues* 14.1 (2007): 1–16.
Al-Jazari. *See* Hill, Donald and Cooraswamy, A. K.
Jazim, M. 'A. al-R. (ed.). *Irtifā' al-dawla al-Mu'ayyadiyya: Jibāyat bilād al-yaman* (Ṣanʿā': Centre français d'archéologie et de sciences sociales, Deutsches Archaologisches Institut, Sanaa branch, 2008).
Kamash, Z. "Irrigation Technology, Society and Environment in the Roman near East," *Journal of Arid Environments* 86 (2012): 65–74.
al-Khazraji, Ali ibn al-Hasan. *The Pearl-Strings: A History of the Résuliyy Dynasty of Yemen*, trans. James W. Redhouse, 5 vols. (Leiden: Brill; London: Luzac, 1906–1919).
King, David A. "Los cuadrantes solares andalusíes," in *El Legado Científico Andalusí* (Madrid: Museo Arqueológico Nacional, 1992), 89–102.
King, David A. "Science in the Service of Religion: The Case of Islam," *Impact of Science on Society* 159 (1990): 245–262.
King, David A. "Three Sundials from Islamic Andalusia," *Journal for the History of Arabic Science* 2.2 (1978): 358–392.
Kirchner, Helena, and Carmen Navarro. "Objectivos, métodos y práctica de la arqueología hidráulica," *Archeologia Medievale* 20 (1993): 121–150.
Knodell, A. R., S. E. Alcock, C. A. Tuttle et al. "The Brown University Petra Archaeological Project: Landscape Archaeology in the Northern Hinterland of Petra, Jordan," *American Journal of Archaeology* 121.4 (2017): 621–683.
Koetsier, Teun, and Hendrik Blauwendraat. "The Archimedean Screw-Pump: A Note on Its Invention and the Development of the Theory," in Marco Ceccarelli (ed.), *Proceedings of the International Symposium on History of Machines and Mechanisms* (New York: Springer, 2004), 181–194.

Kramers, J. H. "Al-Nil," in *Encyclopaedia of Islam*, 2nd ed., 12 vols. Vol. 8 (Leiden: Brill, 1960): 37–43.

Latour, Bruno. *Reassembling the Social: An Introduction to Actor-Network-Theory* (Oxford: Oxford University Press, 2005).

al-Maqqari. *Analectes sur l'histoire et la littérature des arabes d'Espagne*, eds. Reinhart Dozy, Gustave Dugat, Ludolf Krehl, and William Wright, 2 vols. in 3 (Leiden: E. J. Brill, 1855–61; reprinted London: Oriental Press, 1967).

al-Maqqari. *History of the Mohammedan Dynasties in Spain*, ed. and trans. by Pascual de Gayangos, 2 vols. (London: Oriental Translation Fund, 1840–43).

Marçais, Georges. "Sur un lion de marbre trouvé à la Qalʿa des Bani Hammad," *Revue Africaine* 379 (1939): 182–191.

de Miranda, Amanda. *Water Architecture in the Lands of Syria: The Water-Wheels* (Rome: 'L'Erma' di Bretschneider, 2007).

Mirti, Thomas. H., Wesley W. Wallender, William. J. Chancellor, and Mark E. Grismer. "Performance Characteristics of the Shaduf: A Manual Water-Lifting Device," *Applied Engineering in Agriculture* 15.3 (1999): 225–231.

Mostafa, Heba. "The Nile as Nexus: The Nilometer at al-Rawda Island between Veneration and Mediation in Medieval Islamic Egypt," in Katherine Blouin (ed.), *The Nile Delta: Histories from Antiquity to the Modern Period* (Cambridge: Cambridge University Press, 2024), 421–452.

al-Nabulusi. *Ta'rikh al-Fayyum wa-biladihi*, ed. B. Moritz (Cairo: Publications de la Bibliotheque Khediviale, 1898).

Nasir-i Khusraw. *Nasir-i Khusraw's Book of Travels (Safarnama): A Parallel Persian-English text*, ed. and trans. Wheeler Thackston (Costa Mesa: Mazda, 2001).

O'Kane, Bernard. *The Monumental Inscriptions of Historic Cairo*. https://islamicinscriptions.cultnat.org/About.html (accessed March 18, 2024).

Oleson, John P. *Greek and Roman Mechanical Water-Lifting Devices: The History of a Technology* (Dordrecht: D. Reidl, 1984).

Oleson, John P. "Water-Lifting," in Örjan Wikander (ed.), *Handbook of Ancient Water Technology* (Leiden: Brill, 2000), 217–302.

Orihuela Uzal, Antonio, and Carlos Vílchez Vílchez. *Aljibes públicos de la Granada islámica* (Granada: Ayuntamiento de Granada, 1991).

Orihuela Uzal, Antonio and Luis J. García Pulido. "El Suministro de agua en la Granada islámica," in *Ars Mechanica* (S.l.: Ministerior de Fomento, CEDEX-CEHOPU, 2008), 144–149.

Padilla Mellado, Lorenzo L. *Libro del Apeamiento de los Habices del Alpujarra, de las Tahas de Ferreyra, Poqueyra y Jubiles* (Granada: Ayuntamiento de la Alpujarra de la Sierra, 2012).

Pérès, Henri. *Esplendor de al-Andalus: la poesía andaluza en árabe clásico s. XI*, trans. Mercedes García Arenal (Madrid: Hiperión, 1983).
Rapoport, Yossef, and Ido Shahar. "Irrigation in the Medieval Islamic Fayoum: Local Control in a Large-Scale Hydraulic System," *Journal of the Economic and Social History of the* Orient 55 (2012): 1–31.
Remini, Boualem, Jean Albergel, and Bachir Achour. "The Garden Foggara of Timimoun (Algeria): The Decline of Hydraulic Heritage," *Asian Journal of Water, Environment and Pollution* 12.3 (2015): 51–57.
Robinson, Cynthia. *Medieval Andalusian Courtly Culture in the Mediterranean: Ḥadīth Bayāḍ wa Riyāḍ* (New York: Routledge, 2007).
Ruggles, D. Fairchild. "The Aljibe del Rey in Granada," in Anna Bigelow (ed.), *Islam through Objects* (London: Bloomsbury, 2021), 173–188.
Ruggles, D. Fairchild. "The Countryside: The Roman Agricultural and Hydraulic Legacy of the Islamic Mediterranean," in Salma K. Jayyusi, Renata Holod, Attilio Petruccioli, and Andre Raymond (eds.), *The City in the Islamic World*, 2 vols. (Leiden: E. J. Brill, 2008), II: 795–815.
Ruggles, D. Fairchild. "From Garden to Landscape: Lessons from the Taj and the Alhambra," *International Journal of Islamic Architecture* 1.1 (2021): 89–98.
Ruggles, D. Fairchild. "From the Heavens and Hills: The Flow of Water to the Fruited Trees and Ablution Fountains in the Great Mosque of Cordoba," in Sheila Blair and Jonathan Bloom (eds.), *Rivers of Paradise: Water in Islamic Art* (London: Yale University Press, 2009), 81–103.
Ruggles, D. Fairchild. *Gardens, Landscape, and Vision in the Palaces of Islamic Spain* (University Park: Pennsylvania State University Press, 2000).
Ruggles, D. Fairchild. *Islamic Gardens and Landscapes* (Philadelphia: University of Pennsylvania Press, 2008).
Ruggles, D. Fairchild. "Representation, Signature, and Trace in Islamic Art," in Pamela Patton and Henry Schlib (eds.), *The Lives and Afterlives of Medieval Iconography* (University Park: Penn State Press, 2020), 57–86.
Ruggles, D. Fairchild. "The Gardens of the Alhambra and the Concept of the Garden in Islamic Spain" in Jerrilynn D. Dodds (ed.), *Al-Andalus: The Arts of Islamic Spain* (New York: Metropolitan Museum, 1992), 162–171.
Ruggles, D. Fairchild. "Vision and Power at the Qala Bani Hammad in Islamic North Africa," *The Journal of Garden History* 14 (1994): 28–41.
Salameh, Nadim H. "Customary Water Rights in Medieval Wadi Zabid: Some Legal Cases on al-ʿadil biʾl-qanaʿah," *Proceedings of the Seminar for Arabian Studies: Papers from the Thirty-Second Meeting of the Seminar for Arabian Studies held in London, July 16–18, 1998*, 29 (1999): 137–142.

Salameh, Nadim H. "Water Rights in 16th Century Hadramawt – One Question, Two Answers. The Legal Opinions of Ibn Hajar al-Haytami and al-Bakri al-Siddiqi," *Proceedings of the Seminar for Arabian Studies: Papers from the Thirty-Fourth Meeting of the Seminar for Arabian Studies held in London, July 20–22, 2000*, 31 (2001): 215–220.

Samsó, Julio. "Ibn Hišām al-Lajmi y el primer jardín botánico en al-Andalus," *Revista del Instituto Egipcio de Estudios Islámicos en Madrid* 21 (1981–1982): 135–141.

Sato, Tsugitaka. "Irrigation in Rural Egypt from the 12th to the 14th Centuries," *Orient* 8 (1972): 81–92.

Schiøler, Thorkild. *Roman and Islamic Water-Lifting Wheels* (Denmark: Odense University Press, 1971).

Serjeant, R. B. "Some Irrigation Systems in Hadramawt," *Bulletin of the School of Oriental and African Studies* 27.1 (1964): 33–76.

Shaw, Brent D. "Water and Society in the Ancient Maghrib: Technology, Property and Development," *Antiquités Africaines* 20 (1984): 121–173.

Stiros, Stathis C. "Accurate Measurements with Primitive Instruments: The 'paradox' in the qanat design," *Journal of Archaeological Science* 33 (2006): 1058–1064.

Squatriti, Paolo. "Of Seeds, Seasons, and Seas: Andrew Watson's Medieval Agrarian Revolution Forty Years Later," *The Journal of Economic History* 74.4 (2014): 1205–1220.

Torres Balbás, Leopoldo. "La Albolafia de Córdoba y la gran noria toledana," (in Crónica Arqueológica de la España Musulmana XI) *Al-Andalus* 7 (1942): 175–183.

Tribunal de las Aguas de la Vega de Valencia. https://tribunaldelasaguas.org/es/.

Trillo San Jose, Carmen. "A Social Analysis of Irrigation in Al-Andalus: Nazari Granada (13th–15th centuries)," *Journal of Medieval History* 31 (2005): 163–183.

Trillo San José, Carmen. *Agua y Paisaje en Granada* (Granada: Diputación de Granada, 2003).

Trillo San José, Carmen. "Contribución al estudio de la propiedad de la tierra en época nazarí," in Carmen Trillo San José (ed.), *Asentamientos Rurales y Territorio en el Mediterráneo Medieval* (Granada: Athos-Pérgamos, 2002), 499–535.

Trillo San José, Carmen. "Entre Rey y la Comunidad: El Agua del Albaizín (Granada) en la Edad Media," *Meridies: Revista de Historia Medieval* 10 (2012): 151–174.

van Steenbergen, Frank, and Adel al-Weshali, "A New World, More Equity: Changing Water Allocation in Wadi Zabid, Yemen," *The Water Channel*, https://thewaterchannel.tv/thewaterblog/a-new-world-more-equity-changing-water-allocation-in-wadi-zabid-yemen/ (accessed 1 May 2024).

Varisco, Daniel. "Irrigation in an Arabian Valley: A System of Highland Terraces in the Yemen Arab Republic," *Expedition* 25.2 (1983): 26–34.

Varisco, Daniel. *Medieval Agriculture and Islamic Science: The Almanac of a Yemeni Sultan* (Seattle: University of Washington Press, 1994).

Ventura Villanueva, Ángel. *El abastecimiento de agua a la Córdoba romana. I. El Acueducto de Valdepuentes* (Cordoba: Universidad de Córdoba, 1993).

Vitruvius. *The Ten Books on Architecture*, trans. Moris H. Morgan (Cambridge, MA: Harvard University Press, 1914). www.gutenberg.org/files/20239/20239-h/20239-h.htm#CONTENTS.

Watson, Andrew. *Agricultural Innovation in the Early Islamic World: The Diffusion of Crops and Farming Techniques, 700–1100* (Cambridge Studies in Islamic Civilization) (Cambridge: Cambridge University Press, 1983).

Watson, Andrew. "The Arab Agricultural Revolution and Its Diffusion, 700–1100," *The Journal of Economic History* 34.1 (1974): 8–35.

Wescoat, James L. Jr. "Wittfogel East and West: Changing Perspectives on Water Development in South Asia and the United States, 1670–2000," in Alexander Murphy and Douglas Johnson (eds.), *Cultural Encounters with the Environment: Enduring and Evolving Geographic Themes* (Lanham: Rowman and Littlefield, 2000), 109–132.

Whitcomb, Donald Michael Jennings, Andrew Creekmore, and Ignacio Arce. "Khirbet al-Mafjar: New Excavations and Hypotheses for an Umayyad Monument," *Near Eastern Archaeology* 79.2 (2016): 78–87.

Wilkinson, John C. "Muslim Land and Water Law," *Journal of Islamic Studies* 1 (1990): 54–72.

Wilkinson, Tony J. "Settlement, Soil Erosion and Terraced Agriculture in Highland Yemen: A Preliminary Statement," *Proceedings of the Seminar for Arabian Studies* (Papers from the Thirty-Second Meeting of the Seminar for Arabian Studies held in London, July 16–18, 1998) 29 (1999): 183–191.

Wilkinson, Tony J., and Louise Rayne. "Hydraulic Systems in the Middle East," in Helaine Selin (ed.), *Encyclopaedia of the History of Science, Technology, and Medicine in Non-Western Cultures* (Dordrecht: Springer, 2014): 2244–2263. https://doi.org/10.1007/978-94-007-3934-5_10228-1.

Wilson, Andrew. "Classical Water Technology in the Early Islamic World," in Christer Bruun and Ari Saastamoinen (eds.), *Technology, Ideology, Water: From Frontinus to the Renaissance and beyond* (Acta Instituti Romani Finlandiae, 31) (Rome: Finnish Institute in Rome, 2004), 115–141.

Wilson, Andrew. "Water Supply in Ancient Carthage," in J. T. Peña, J. J. Rossiter, A. I. Wilson et al. (eds.), *Carthage Papers* (*Journal of Roman Archaeology*, Supplementary series 28) (Portsmouth, 1998), 65–102.

Wilson, Andrew, David Mattingly, and Martin Sterry. "The Diffusion of Irrigation Technologies in the Sahara in Antiquity," in Chloé Duckworth, Aurélie Cuénod, and David Mattingly (eds.), *Mobile Technologies in the Ancient Sahara and beyond* (Cambridge: Cambridge University Press, 2020), 68–114.

Wittfogel, Karl. *Oriental Despotism: A Comparative Study of Total Power* (New Haven: Yale University Press, 1957).

Zaqzouq, Abdul Razzak. "Les Norias: Anciens Moyens d'Irrigation les Plus Importants dans la Région de Hama," in Bernard Geyer (ed.), *Techniques et Pratiques Hydro-Agricoles Traditionelles en Domaine Irrigué (Actes de Colloque de Damas, 27 juin -1 juillet 1987)*, 2 vols. (Paris: Librarie Orientaliste Paul Geunther, 1990), II: 337–365.

Acknowledgements

My thanks to Geraldine Heng who first suggested this volume. At the University of Illinois, Urbana-Champaign, master's student Maija Mallula created some of the drawings, adding to those made by previous students Lobsang Chodon, Barbara Schleicher, and Binaifer Variava. Helga Varden, Luca Galuzzi, and Felix Arnold kindly allowed me to reproduce their plans and photos. My thanks also to Ingrid Hehmeyer for her inspiring work and her kindness in helping me obtain the Wadi Zabid canal diagram. I completed the book with support as the Debra L. Mitchell Chair in Landscape Architecture and a sabbatical leave from the University of Illinois.

I traced the course of some of the canals discussed in this volume in the company of hiking companions in Andalucia: Jonathan Druker, Basel Hajeb, Luis José García Pulido, Cameron McCarthy, Lucas Meza-Bettivia, Lisa Rosenthal, Angharad Valdivia, Helga Varden, Jürgen Varden, Oscar Vázquez, Shelley Weinberg, Thomas Woltz.

In travels and in life, Oscar Vázquez is my beloved companion and I dedicate this book to him.

Cambridge Elements

The Global Middle Ages

Geraldine Heng
University of Texas at Austin

Geraldine Heng is Perceval Professor of English and Comparative Literature at the University of Texas, Austin. She is the author of *The Invention of Race in the European Middle Ages* (2018) and *England and the Jews: How Religion and Violence Created the First Racial State in the West* (2018), both published by Cambridge University Press, as well as *Empire of Magic: Medieval Romance and the Politics of Cultural Fantasy* (2003, Columbia). She is the editor of *Teaching the Global Middle Ages* (2022, MLA), coedits the University of Pennsylvania Press series, RaceB4Race: Critical Studies of the Premodern, and is working on a new book, *Early Globalisms: The Interconnected World, 500–1500 CE*. Originally from Singapore, Heng is a Fellow of the Medieval Academy of America, a member of the Medievalists of Color, and Founder and Co-director, with Susan Noakes, of the Global Middle Ages Project: www.globalmiddleages.org.

Susan J. Noakes
University of Minnesota–Twin Cities

Susan J. Noakes is Professor of French and Italian at the University of Minnesota – Twin Cities, where she also serves as Chair of the Department of French and Italian. For her many publications in French, Italian, and comparative literature, the university in 2009 named her Inaugural Chair in Arts, Design, and Humanities. Her most recent publication is an analysis of Salim Bachi's *L'Exil d'Ovide*, exploring a contemporary writer's reflection on his exile to Europe by comparing it to Ovid's exile to the Black Sea; it appears in *Salim Bachi*, edited by Agnes Schaffhauser, published in Paris by Harmattan in 2020.

Lynn Ramey
Vanderbilt University

Lynn Ramey is Professor of French and Cinema and Media Arts at Vanderbilt University and Chair of the Department of French and Italian. She is the author of *Jean Bodel: An Introduction* (2024, University Press of Florida), *Black Legacies: Race and the European Middle Ages* (2014, University Press of Florida), and *Christian, Saracen and Genre in Medieval French Literature* (2001, Routledge). She is currently working on recreations of medieval language, literature, and culture in video games for which she was awarded an NEH digital humanities advancement grant in 2022.

About the Series
Elements in the Global Middle Ages is a series of concise studies that introduce researchers and instructors to an uncentered, interconnected world, c. 500–1500 CE. Individual Elements focus on the globe's geographic zones, its natural and built environments, its cultures, societies, arts, technologies, peoples, ecosystems, and lifeworlds.

Cambridge Elements =

The Global Middle Ages

Elements in the Series

Southeast Asian Interconnections: Geography, Networks and Trade
Derek Heng

Slavery in East Asia
Don J. Wyatt

Early Tang China and the World, 618–750 CE
Shao-yun Yang

Late Tang China and the World, 750–907 CE
Shao-yun Yang

Medieval Textiles across Eurasia, c. 300–1400
Patricia Blessing, Elizabeth Dospěl Williams and Eiren L. Shea

The Chertsey Tiles, the Crusades, and Global Textile Motifs
Amanda Luyster

Swahili Worlds in Globalism
Chapurukha M. Kusimba

"Ethiopia" and the World, 330–1500 CE
Yonatan Binyam and Verena Krebs

Global Ships: Seafaring, Shipwrecks, and Boatbuilding in the Global Middle Ages
Amanda Respess

Elephants and Ivory in China and Spain
John Beusterien and Stephen West

The Global Legend of Prester John
Christopher E. Taylor

Islamicate Environments: Water, Land, Plants, and Society
D. Fairchild Ruggles

A full series listing is available at: www.cambridge.org/EGMA

For EU product safety concerns, contact us at Calle de José Abascal, 56–1°, 28003 Madrid, Spain or eugpsr@cambridge.org.